CHARLES F. STANLEY BIBLE STUDY SERIES

OVERCOMING THE ENEMY

LIVE IN VICTORY OVER
TRIALS AND TEMPTATIONS

CHARLES F. STANLEY

THOMAS NELSON
Since 1798

Overcoming the Enemy
Charles F. Stanley Bible Study Series

Copyright © 1996, 2008, 2020 by Charles F. Stanley.

Published in Nashville, Tennessee, by Thomas Nelson. Thomas Nelson is a registered trademark of HarperCollins Christian Publishing, Inc.

All Scripture quotations are taken from the New King James Version.® Copyright © 1982 by Thomas Nelson. Used by permission. All rights reserved worldwide.

Thomas Nelson titles may be purchased in bulk for educational, business, fundraising, or sales promotional use. For information, e-mail SpecialMarkets@ThomasNelson.com.

ISBN 978-0-310-10560-2 (softcover)
ISBN 978-0-310-10561-9 (ebook)

First Printing February 2020 / Printed in the United States of America

CONTENTS

Preparing to Overcome the Enemy

Many people in the world today believe that the devil does not exist. They believe that he is merely an ancient myth—a metaphor to explain the presence of evil in our world. But the Bible teaches clearly that the devil is real . . . and that he wants to destroy us.

This is the bad news. The good news is that Jesus has already defeated the devil—utterly, permanently, and irrevocably. Of course, this does not mean that we will never be confronted by the enemy of our soul. On the contrary, the devil is still actively seeking our harm. But the power of Jesus Christ is all we need to defeat the devil every time he attacks.

This book can be used by you alone or by several people in a small-group study. At various times, you will be asked to relate to the material in one of the following four ways.

First, what new insights have you gained? Make notes about the insights you have. You may want to record them in your Bible or in a separate journal. As you reflect on your new understanding, you are likely to see how God has moved in your life.

Second, have you ever had a similar experience? You approach the Bible from your own unique background . . . your own particular set of understandings about the world that you bring with you when you open God's Word. For this reason, it is important to consider how your experiences are shaping your understanding and allow yourself to be open to the truth that God reveals.

Third, how do you feel about the material? While you should not depend solely on your emotions as a gauge for your faith, it is important for you to be aware of them as you study a passage of Scripture and can freely express them to God. Sometimes, the Holy Spirit will use your emotions to compel you to look at your life in a different or challenging way.

Fourth, in what way do you feel challenged to respond or to act? God's Word may inspire you or challenge you to take a particular action. Take this challenge seriously and find ways to move into it. If God reveals a particular need that He wants you to address, take that as His "marching orders." God will empower you to do something with the challenge that He has just given you.

Start your Bible study sessions in prayer. Ask God to give you spiritual eyes to see and spiritual ears to hear. As you conclude your study, ask the Lord to seal what you have learned so you will not forget it. Ask Him to help you grow into the fullness of the nature and character of Christ Jesus.

I encourage you to keep the Bible at the center of your study. A genuine Bible study stays focused on God's Word and promotes a growing faith and a closer walk with the Holy Spirit in each person who participates.

Our Foremost Enemy

IN THIS LESSON

Learning: Is the devil real?

Growing: Who would want to harm me spiritually?

Believers in Christ Jesus have three main enemies in life: *the world, the flesh,* and *the devil.* These enemies are constantly present to harass us, create conflict for us, and generate trouble for us. Although we cannot escape these enemies completely, we are assured of victory over them as long as we rely on the Lord Jesus for our wisdom, power, and ability to endure.

The *world* includes anything of a physical nature that might hinder us in our walk with Christ or tempt us to sin. Contrary to what some people think, the world is not getting better. If anything it is getting worse, because so many more possibilities for evil exist today than hundreds or thousands of years ago—the world has more people, greater opportunities for evil alliances and evil behavior, more technology for delivering tempting messages, more information about how to engage in evil, and more varieties of false religions. The ways and means for committing evil have exploded, not diminished.

The *flesh* has to do with the nature of the human heart, which has not changed since the creation of man. The human heart still has a bent toward darkness, evil, and sin. We have desires that God wants us to meet in ways that are in keeping with His commandments. However, the temptation always exists for us to meet those desires in ways that are ungodly. We never lose our human, fleshly desires, and we never lose our capacity to yield to temptation. These desires are with us until we die, because they reside within us.

Peter described the *devil* this way: "Your adversary the devil walks about like a roaring lion, seeking whom he may devour" (1 Peter 5:8). Each of us—whether we realize it or not—faces a spiritual battle with the devil today. The very nature of the enemy is to defeat us, to destroy us, and to kill everything that is important to us (see John 10:10). His pursuit of us is persistent, unrelenting, and always aimed at the most vulnerable area of our lives.

1. Why does Peter describe the devil as your adversary? What images come to mind when you think of the devil as a "roaring lion"?

2. Why might some people think the devil does not exist? What does the Bible teach?

A LESSON IN SPIRITUAL WARFARE

Jesus had to continually battle these spiritual enemies throughout His ministry. One of the first events that occurred in Jesus' ministry was His baptism by John in the Jordan River. Luke writes, "It came to pass that Jesus also was baptized; and while He prayed, the heaven was opened. And the Holy Spirit descended in bodily form like a dove upon Him, and a voice came from heaven which said, 'You are My beloved Son; in You I am well pleased'" (3:21–22).

Immediately after this high point in Jesus' life, we find the Holy Spirit leading Jesus into a wilderness. Luke tells us the reason for this journey: "Then Jesus, being filled with the Holy Spirit, returned from the Jordan and was led by the Spirit into the wilderness, being tempted for forty days by the devil. And in those days He ate nothing, and afterward, when they had ended, He was hungry" (4:1–2).

I am sure that Satan tempted Jesus when He was a child growing up in Nazareth. We know for a fact that Satan tempted Jesus during this time of fasting in the wilderness. In truth, Satan tempted Jesus throughout His ministry. In Luke's account, we read that "when the devil had ended every temptation, he departed from Him until an opportune time" (verse 13). Satan departed from Jesus because he had been told to leave . . . but only for a season.

Jesus had to frequently battle the forces of the *world* in the form of the Jewish religious leaders and Roman authorities. He battled the forces of the *flesh,* for "we do not have a High Priest who cannot sympathize with our weaknesses, but was in all points tempted as we are, yet without sin" (Hebrews 4:15). He was continually under attack by the *devil,* who tried everything to get Jesus to abandon His mission and avoid the cross. Jesus once even recognized Satan using His disciple Peter to try to acheive this goal. When Peter tried to tell Jesus that He would not be crucified, Christ responded, "Get behind Me, Satan! You are an offense to Me, for you are not mindful of the things of God, but the things of men" (Matthew 16:23).

Satan's last-ditch effort occurred in the Garden of Gethsemane. He was there, whispering to Jesus, "You can avert this. You can avoid this. You can accomplish the same purposes without having to go to the cross. You don't have to do this." As Luke relates, "Coming out, He went to the Mount of Olives, as He was accustomed, and His disciples also followed Him. When He came to the place, He said to them, 'Pray that you may not enter into temptation'" (Luke 22:39–40). Jesus knew that Satan was already working on Him.

However, in the end Jesus said, "Father, if it is Your will, take this cup away from Me; nevertheless not My will, but Yours, be done" (verse 42). Jesus submitted His will to that of God the Father—and secured the eternal victory. The same will be true of us when we submit our desires to God and rely on His strength for the victory.

3. "Jesus, being filled with the Holy Spirit, returned from the Jordan and was led by the Spirit into the wilderness" (Luke 4:1). Why do you think the Holy Spirit led Jesus into the desert when He knew that Jesus would be tested there?

4. "Count it all joy when you fall into various trials, knowing that the testing of your faith produces patience" (James 1:2–3). Why can you "count it all joy" when you face trials? What can these trials—with the help of the Holy Spirit—produce within you?

....

....

....

....

....

....

....

....

A Need for Daily Victory

Just as in Jesus' time, the world, the flesh, and the devil are still with us. So, our best recourse is to learn how to deal with them and have *daily* victory over them. It would be wonderful if we could defeat these enemies once and for all, but this isn't a provision God has made. Instead, He has provided us with the Holy Spirit, who resides within us to help us in our struggle.

Jesus described the work of the Holy Spirit when He said to His disciples, "These things I have spoken to you while being present with you. But the Helper, the Holy Spirit, whom the Father will send in My name, He will teach you all things, and bring to your remembrance all things that I said to you" (John 14:25–26). The Holy Spirit gives us the ability to say *no* to the temptations of the world and to overcome our fleshly desires. The Holy Spirit also enables us to withstand the assaults of the devil on a day-to-day basis and experience peace and wholeness even in the face of severe spiritual opposition.

We face a daily struggle, but we can also experience daily victories. God calls us to live one day at a time. We will not have a single, definitive showdown with the devil in our lives—a moment in which he is defeated and made unable to accuse or torment us again—but we can experience a *daily* victory over the devil. We can say no to the temptations he presents *today*. We can use our faith to defeat his assault against our minds, bodies, and spirits *today*. We can pray against his efforts to destroy us *today*. A string of daily victories makes a victorious life!

5. "The flesh lusts against the Spirit, and the Spirit against the flesh; and these are contrary to one another, so that you do not do the things that you wish" (Galatians 5:17). What does it mean that "the flesh lusts against the Spirit"? Give practical examples.

....

....

....

....

....

....

....

....

....

6. In what sense is the Spirit contrary to the flesh? Why must a Christian deny one—flesh or Spirit—in order to indulge the other?

....

....

....

....

....

....

....

....

....

An Assurance of Victory

As we will discuss in this study, we battle against the world and the flesh by first learning how to discern God's will in a given situation and then by having the courage to say no to evil. These battles are won or lost on the battleground of our physical, material, and emotional lives. It is an *ongoing* battle to overcome the world and the flesh because the devil—the enemy of our souls—is behind these battles. Ultimately, our battle in each of these areas is spiritual in nature. It is waged in the spirit, and it has eternal and far-reaching spiritual consequences.

The devil's purpose is not simply to irritate us or make our lives difficult. His goal is to destroy us in the spiritual realm. The devil will use whatever is made available to him as a toehold on which to establish his evil purposes. His ultimate goal is to annihilate us—physically, materially, emotionally, mentally, and spiritually.

However, as we focus on this spiritual warfare, we will do so from the perspective that the devil is a defeated foe. Of course, we cannot defeat him by our own authority—rather, he has been defeated by Christ. Jesus referred to the devil as the "ruler of this world" (John 12:31), and He said of him, "he has nothing in Me" (John 14:30). The devil has no authority, power, or influence over Jesus. The book of Revelation graphically details Jesus' definitive victory over the devil when He casts him "into the lake of fire and brimstone," where the devil "will be tormented day and night forever and ever" (20:10).

This may lead you to ask, "If the devil is defeated, why do we still have to fight?" The victory over the devil is assured in reality, *but it is not yet accomplished in time.* The fate of the devil is sealed, but he still has access to humankind until the day when God brings this age to an end. The existence of the devil is related to our having free will as human beings. God has given human beings the ability to choose . . . and that includes our ability to choose evil. The devil, as the supreme agent of evil, has the power to tempt us and to oppress us.

What we do know with certainty is that *whenever* the devil is confronted with Jesus, the Lord Jesus wins. When we place our faith and hope in Christ and resist the devil, the devil cannot score a victory over us. We may lose battles against the devil from time to time, but *we will not lose the war* because we belong to Christ. It is important to keep this assurance of victory at the forefront of our thinking as we study spiritual warfare. If we look only at the devil and his tactics, it is easy to become discouraged or fearful. But if we keep our focus on Jesus Christ, however, we remain strong and alive in our spirits.

7. "Do not love the world or the things in the world. If anyone loves the world, the love of the Father is not in him" (1 John 2:15). What does it mean to love the world?

8. Why is love of the world incompatible with love of God?

THE GREAT VALUE
OF CHRISTIAN ALLIES

Everyone faces spiritual battles. And every person alive knows what it means to come up against the devil's assaults. For this reason, this is an area in our Christian walk in which each of us should have great empathy toward our brothers and sisters in Christ.

One of our greatest privileges and responsibilities is to help our fellow believers fight and win spiritual battles. No person is intended to confront the devil alone. Christ assures us that He is always present. Even so, we are to function as the *body* of Christ, one to another. We are to join forces with those who are under attack by the enemy and become fellow warriors, doing battle in the spirit realm through our prayers and loving support.

As we face spiritual battles, we are wise to turn to our brothers and sisters in Christ and ask for their help. As we see others facing spiritual battles, we are admonished by the Bible to go to them and help them win a victory through Christ. We are to fight against our common enemy, Satan, and his demons. Imagine how much would be accomplished in our churches today if believers would band together against their true enemy rather than wasting their time and energy bickering with one another or fighting against matters of lesser importance!

So I encourage you to see your Bible-study group and your fellow Christians as a band of God's warriors, powerfully equipped for battle through your relationship with Christ Jesus and your empowerment by the Holy Spirit. Expect your study of the Word to equip you to help one another as you continue to build your relationship with other believers in your church or community, even after this study has ended.

9. "Let the word of Christ dwell in you richly in all wisdom, teaching and admonishing one another in psalms and hymns and spiritual songs, singing with grace in your hearts to the Lord" (Colossians 3:16). To *admonish* means to warn and guide another back to the right path. What are some ways you are admonishing your fellow believers in Christ?

....

....

....

....

....

....

10. "Let us consider one another in order to stir up love and good works, not forsaking the assembling of ourselves together, as is the manner of some, but exhorting one another" (Hebrews 10:24–25). Why do you think the Bible stresses the importance of believers joining together and doing life together? What strength does this provide to a believer?

....

....

....

....

....

....

TODAY AND TOMORROW

Today: The devil is real, but Jesus has utterly defeated him.

Tomorrow: I will ask the Lord to help me see where I can strengthen my spiritual life this week.

CLOSING PRAYER

Heavenly Father, thank You for promising to be with us as we confront the enemies of the world, the flesh, and the devil. We know these forces are constantly present to harass us, but as we rely on Your strength, we can be assured of the victory. Thank You also for Your comforting words that You set limitations on our temptations so that we can bear them successfully, victoriously, and triumphantly. We pray that the Holy Spirit will help each of us to examine our lives and evaluate what really is going on—and rely on the promise that Jesus Christ came to set us free from bondage and the snares of the enemy.

Notes and Prayer Requests

Use this space to write any key points, questions, or prayer requests from this week's study.

THE NATURE OF OUR ENEMY

IN THIS LESSON

Learning: Just who is the devil?

Growing: What can the devil do to me?

One of the foremost rules of warfare is to know your enemy. The more you know about your enemy—how he thinks and what motivates him—the more you are to defeat him. To overcome the enemy of our eternal spirit, the first thing we must know about him is his nature.

Peter described the devil as a "roaring lion, seeking whom he may devour" (1 Peter 5:8). Most big-game hunters consider the lion to be the most dangerous of animals. It is extremely powerful and can move quick and low (out of sight in tall grassland areas). It has a great ability to track its prey, being stealthy in its maneuvers and deceptive in its motives. A lion's awesome roar instills fear that often paralyzes its prey, making conquest all the easier.

Peter accurately identified all these characteristics with the devil. The devil is powerful, deceptive, and secretive, and he can act swiftly if given an opportunity. His roar against us can cause us to quake in fear. Peter was writing to Christians who were enduring great persecution, and they readily understood this graphic image. The enemies of Christianity often operated secretly. The early Christians knew they had enemies waiting to pounce on them for their faith, but the enemies' identity was often unknown to the Christians.

Peter also said the devil shows no favoritism when he attacks: "The same sufferings are experienced by your brotherhood in the world" (1 Peter 5:9). The devil acts like a roaring lion toward believers and unbelievers alike. His behavior doesn't change according to his prey—it is his nature to be like a roaring lion, seeking whom he may devour. A lion's actions are consistent whether its prey is a wildebeest or a young zebra. A lion always acts like a lion.

The devil is often depicted humorously as an imp with a pitchfork sitting on a person's shoulder and whispering naughty things into his ear. Nothing could be farther from the truth. The devil is always seeking our destruction. He is forever on the prowl and never satisfied with his most recent kill. Jesus said the devil comes at us with the purposes of stealing anything of value, killing our relationships, and destroying our health and our lives (see John 10:10).

The devil is a fierce opponent. There is nothing humorous about his tactics or his intent, and there certainly is nothing to laugh about if we are his intended victims. We do ourselves a serious disservice if we discount his existence, take him lightly, or believe we are capable of defeating him in our own strength.

1. "He [the devil] was a murderer from the beginning, and does not stand in the truth, because there is no truth in him. When he speaks a lie, he speaks from his own resources, for he is a liar and

the father of it" (John 8:44). What characteristics does Jesus reveal about the devil in this verse?

....

....

....

....

....

....

....

2. How do these character traits differ from the world's views of the devil?

....

....

....

....

....

....

....

OTHER DESCRIPTIONS OF THE ENEMY

As noted previously, Peter called the devil an *adversary*, or someone who seeks to oppose us. Adversaries may oppose what we say or do, or they may be hostile toward us simply because we exist. Adversaries will take a stand against us no matter what we do or don't do. Satan's goal is to defeat us because he *wants* to defeat us. He takes personal pleasure in doing so.

This means we don't have to *do* anything to earn the devil's hatred. By the contrariness of his very nature, he is opposed even to those who serve him. He entices and then kills his victims, often with the very thing he used to entice them. We see this all the time in our world today. People are enticed to use drugs and alcohol, and then many of them die from related diseases, accidents, or overdoses. Others turn to occult practices, only to become the victims of those same practices. Many people are drawn to crave material goods and then pay a high penalty for stealing or embezzling.

Some people believe the devil likes particular people and gives them certain powers. The devil has never liked *any* human being. Every one of us is a potential threat to him. The devil uses people the way a cat plays with a mouse just prior to eating it. The devil has disliked us from our birth, solely because we are God's creations designed with a specific purpose that is ultimately for our good and God's glory. The devil doesn't want us to bring glory to God or live a life that points toward His love. He will never cease to be our adversary.

The Bible has other names for the devil, each of which describe various aspects of his evil nature: *tempter* (see Matthew 4:3); *Beelzebub*, a ruler of maggots and agent of decay (see 12:27); *Satan*, the one who brings continual accusation against those who have faith in God (see 12:26), *father of lies* (see John 8:44); *thief* (see 10:10), and *deceiver* (see Revelation 12:9). None of these names are flattering! There is not one ounce of good in him. He is evil to the core.

3. "The thief does not come except to steal, and to kill, and to destroy. I have come that they may have life, and that they may have it more abundantly" (John 10:10). What are the devil's goals for your life? What are Jesus' goals?

....

....

....

....

....

....

....

....

4. When have you seen the powers of the world lead to death or destruction in your life or someone you love? How did the end result differ from the beginning temptation?

....

....

....

....

....

THE ENEMY'S GOALS

The devil is always prowling around your life. His tactics are like that of a pride of lions—to zero in on a weakness, divide, and destroy. When the devil thinks he has an opening, he attacks. You will usually have a general awareness the devil is not far away, but there are times when you will be keenly aware he is making a direct move against you. This is a *satanic attack*.

If you are a believer, the devil cannot destroy your relationship with Christ. He cannot cross the blood barrier that Jesus purchased on your behalf when He died on the cross. In Christ, you have eternal life (see John 3:16; 1 John 5:11–13). Paul wrote that neither principalities nor powers could separate you from God's love (see Romans 8:38). *Principalities* and *powers* describe demonic forces. Paul also said neither height nor depth could separate you from Christ (see verse 39). *Depth* refers in part to *Sheol*—the place of the dead.

However, what the devil can do is attack you in the realm of your emotions, your mind, and your body. He can move against you so you no longer have the energy, the health, the drive, or even much of a desire to serve God. The devil cannot score a definitive victory over you . . . but he can render you ineffective.

The devil can also attack your reputation and your witness. He always is seeking a means of destroying the testimony of a Christian—again in order to render that Christian ineffective for the gospel's sake.

The devil knows he can't take away the eternal life of a believer, but he will do his best to make the believer *useless* as an advocate for God's kingdom on earth. In other words, the devil may not be able to keep you from heaven, but he will do his best to make certain that you don't take anybody to heaven with you.

Satan is committed to destroying you at any cost. He is patient and willing to wait for the one moment of weakness that he needs to attack you. He is also persistent and will not give up seeking your destruction. You would be unwise if you think you can ever have a respite from the devil or think you can conquer him once and for all in your life—or even in one particular area of your life. He continues to prowl, to wait, to watch, and to seek a basis to attack you.

If Satan can't influence you directly, he will attempt to influence others around you in order to divert your attention from Christ or weaken your resolve to walk in purity with Christ. The only way to ensure that he does not gain an opportunity in your life is to remain close to Christ and to walk daily in the guidance and strength offered to you by the Holy Spirit. You have to maintain your resolve to say *no* to the temptation to sin and to seek God's forgiveness quickly anytime you fail to keep His commandments.

5. "For I am persuaded that neither death nor life, nor angels nor principalities nor powers, nor things present nor things to come, nor height nor depth, nor any other created thing, shall be able to separate us from the love of God which is in Christ Jesus our Lord" (Romans 8:38–39). What does this say about God's love for you? Is there anything *not* covered by this list when it comes to what can separate you from God's love?

6. What do these verses suggest when it comes to the attacks of the devil? How do they assure you that because of Christ, you will have the ultimate victory over the enemy?

....

....

....

....

....

....

THE LIMITS OF THE ENEMY'S POWER

As powerful and cunning as Satan may be, he is neither omnipotent (all-powerful) nor omniscient (all-knowing) like the Lord. In fact, the devil bears none of the absolute or everlasting qualities of God. The devil was originally called Lucifer, and he was one of the archangels of heaven. As a created being, he had a beginning—and he will have a horrible ending: destruction and torment in a lake of fire and brimstone (see Revelation 20:10).

As a created being, the devil is also not omnipresent—he can only be in one place at a time. Many people believe they are doing constant battle with Satan, but in all likelihood, they have never had a single battle with Satan himself. The forces they have battled are Satan's *demons*—the fallen angels who joined Lucifer in rebelling against God. It is primarily through demons that Satan exerts his influence on human beings.

Demons have the ability to tempt. They have the ability to torment and oppress, including the ability to harass Christians. Paul described demonic activity with Christians as a wrestling match (see Ephesians 6:11-12). Satan himself does not indwell human beings, for to do so would limit his power. However, demons have the ability to indwell a non-Christian so the person begins to act the same way Satan would act if he were present on the scene.

The demons are organized and ruled by Satan. They do what he commands. The Bible tells us the forces of darkness have a hierarchy. As we have seen, Paul described this as "principalities . . . powers . . . rulers of the darkness" (Ephesians 6:12). Demonic activity is widespread and constant. In fact, John wrote, "the whole world lies under the sway of the wicked one" (1 John 5:19). The devil exercises his influence through his demons.

Satan and his demonic forces are powerful and prevalent, but they are not sovereign. Only God is sovereign. Only God possesses ultimate authority over His universe. Satan cannot exceed the limits that God has put on him, and neither can his demons. God may allow Satan an opportunity to tempt or to exert influence in a person's life, but God determines the extent to which Satan can operate. God retains ultimate control . . . always.

We see this in the life of Job. Satan asked for access to torment him, and God allowed him to do so (see Job 1:6–12; 2:1–6). The first time Satan made this request, God said, "Behold, all that he has is in your power; only do not lay a hand on his person" (1:12). Satan caused the death of Job's sons and daughters, as well as the loss of Job's herds, flocks, and servants. Yet Job responded by saying, "The LORD gave, and the LORD has taken away; blessed be the name of the LORD" (1:21). He did not blame God for any of his misfortune. The second time Satan asked permission to tempt Job, the Lord said, "Behold, he is in your hand, but spare his life" (2:6).

This story reveals two important points about the limits of Satan's power. *First, Satan is subservient to God.* He can bring accusations against a person and can question God, but he cannot touch the person who fears God and shuns evil unless God gives him permission (see 1:1). *Second, God puts limits on what Satan is allowed to do.* Satan cannot overstep the boundaries that God puts on him. At the end of Job's story, God says to Job, "Who then is able to stand against

Me? Who has preceded Me, that I should pay him? Everything under heaven is Mine" (41:10–11). *Everything* includes, of course, Satan and his demons.

Part of the deception Satan has played on the minds of men and women is that he is as powerful as God, that he is equal to God, and that he holds just as much power for evil as God holds for good. This simply is not true. Satan operates *under* God's sovereignty. He is a rebel against a higher authority. God alone is the sovereign King of the universe, and He has no equal.

7. "If we say that we have no sin, we deceive ourselves, and the truth is not in us. If we confess our sins, He is faithful and just to forgive us our sins and to cleanse us from all unrighteousness" (1 John 1:8–9). How does Satan sometimes deceive people into denying sin? When have you seen this in your own life?

....

....

....

....

....

....

....

8. What do you learn about the limits of Satan's power from the story of God? What do you learn about the power that God holds?

....

....

....

....

....

....

....

....

OUR RESPONSE TO THE ENEMY

What should our response be to the devil once we know his nature? I believe we should have a clear understanding of the devil's power, but as Christians we should not cower in fear before him. He is a defeated foe—Christ Jesus, our Lord, is victor over him. The person who does not have a personal relationship with Jesus is the one who should fear the devil. That person has no shield against the devil and is open prey to the devil's assaults.

If you have not accepted Christ as your personal Savior but are not walking closely with Him today, I encourage you to own up to your sinful nature and recognize that you are living apart from God. Accept Jesus' payment for your sins, ask the Father to forgive you and transform your sin nature, and ask Him to fill you with His Holy Spirit so that you might live a life that is pleasing to Him. Unless you are a Christian, you cannot overcome the enemy of your soul. As long as you are a nonbeliever, you are one of the devil's favorite targets. You are destined to be his victim without any recourse as long as you remain in rebellion against God.

9. "For He says: 'In an acceptable time I have heard you, and in the day of salvation I have helped you.' Behold, now is the accepted time; behold, now is the day of salvation" (2 Corinthians 6:2). Have you accepted Jesus as your Lord and Savior? If not, what is preventing you from doing so right now?

10. If you have accepted Christ as your Savior, how are you protected from the devil?

....

....

....

....

....

....

TODAY AND TOMORROW

Today: Satan cannot touch a hair of my head
without God's permission.

Tomorrow: I will place my faith completely in Christ
to protect me from the devil's attacks.

CLOSING PRAYER

Father, thank You for your wonderful love, goodness, and mercy toward us. Thank You for making us aware of the nature and tactics of the enemy that we face every day. Today, we pray that You will grant clarity to those who are undergoing temptation right now—who have been toying, playing, reasoning, and rationalizing with the devil's lies—to help them see what Satan has really been doing. Given them the wisdom and the strength to get on their knees right now, turn their back on that temptation, and surrender afresh and anew to You as the Lord of their lives.

NOTES AND PRAYER REQUESTS

Use this space to write any key points, questions, or prayer requests from this week's study.

THE TACTICS OF OUR ENEMY

IN THIS LESSON

Learning: Why do I wind up committing sin
when I don't want to?

Growing: How can I prevent temptation
before it gets started?

We need to not only know the nature of the enemy but also understand his tactics. A knowledge of the devil's methods will equip us to discern when the devil is at work and to know how to resist him and withstand his assaults. Satan's primary tool is *deception*. He works in our minds to get us to call good "bad" and bad "good." He is a master of twisting the truth and veiling what is harmful so that it *appears* to be beneficial.

The devil is an expert at appearances, disguises, and illusions. He is the master counterfeiter. The best counterfeits, of course, are those that are most like the genuine articles. The devil specializes in "good fakes." He comes at us in a way that is appealing and appears to be spiritual and acceptable. Paul referred to him as an "angel of light" who is *masquerading* as one of God's holy angels: "For Satan himself transforms himself into an angel of light. Therefore it is no great thing if his ministers [demons] also transform themselves into ministers of righteousness, whose end will be according to their works" (2 Corinthians 11:14–15).

Satan achieves his goals when a person *appears* to be doing something that is good or noble but in fact is operating from *evil motives* and for *evil ends*. Ultimately, the darkness in an evil person will be revealed and will destroy him or her. Unfortunately, this will often not occur until many others are deceived and are living according to Satan's purposes.

Satan's best human agents are "successful" people who claim they have made their way in life totally on their own intellect and skill, who refuse to acknowledge Jesus Christ, and who are fountains of all sorts of false philosophies. They operate in a wide variety of religions and "isms" around the world—including the religions of secularism and humanism, which worship the idols of human achievement. These expert agents of Satan appear to be well-intentioned and claim to have the needs and concerns of others at heart. In reality, they are self-centered, godless people who are motivated by a greed for possessions and a lust for personal power.

The more Satan watches us and knows us, the more veiled his tactics become toward us. He rarely will attack us head-on at our strong points. Rather, he will discover our weaknesses and bore into us over time, chipping away at our lives with persistence and increasing subtlety. It's as if he says, "Well, they saw through that and didn't buy my lie, so let me see if I can hide my intent a little and try another tactic that won't be so easily recognized." The more we resist the devil, the more clever and veiled the devil's deceptions will be. Over time, this can reach the point where, as Jesus said, even the strongest and most committed Christians can be in danger of becoming deceived (see Matthew 24:24).

1. When have you been deceived into thinking something bad was good, or vice versa?

2. What are some examples of good things the world calls *bad* and some bad things that the world calls *good*?

THE ENEMY PLANTS AN IDEA

There are several identifiable stages to the deception that Satan employs. *First, he plants an idea in our imaginations.* Everybody has an imagination. It is a part of our thinking that we use for exploring "what if" possibilities and dreams. The imagination is neutral—it can be turned to bad or good. Those who use their imaginations for good can be a positive force for building up God's people and expanding the kingdom of God on earth. Such people can envision highly innovative ways to spread the gospel and show God's love to those who are desperately in need of it. On the other hand, those who allow their imaginations to be used for evil can have an equally dangerous and damaging influence on others.

We must ask about any new idea, "Where will the implementation of this lead?" In other words, will the implementation of the idea point us and others to heaven? Or will it lead us or others astray and cause us to be detoured away from godly matters? The devil loves to implant ideas that have an appealing element. He knows what we like and what we want in our fleshly desires, so wraps up his temptation in something that we find attractive. He does this so we will at least entertain the idea a while. We may call it a fantasy, daydream, or wish. We know it is wrong, but we assume there is no harm because we are only *thinking about it.*

The more we dwell on one of Satan's ideas, the more we are trapped by it. We sometimes say that certain things or ideas *capture* our imaginations. In fact, they do! The longer an idea is entertained in the imagination, the more likely we are to act on it.

3. "For the weapons of our warfare are not carnal but mighty in God for pulling down strongholds, casting down arguments and every high thing that exalts itself against the knowledge of God, bringing every thought into captivity to the obedience of Christ" (2 Corinthians 10:4–5). What are the "weapons of our warfare"?

4. What does it mean to bring every thought into captivity? How is this done?

....

....

....

....

....

....

....

....

WE IDENTIFY WITH THE IDEA

Once an idea has been planted in our imagination, we begin to identify with it. We start to put ourselves into the picture. We wonder how it would feel to own that object or to be with that person or participate in that activity. The longer we identify with the idea, the more we *desire* to try it out. We begin to dwell on the idea, and it occupies more and more of our mental energy. Increasingly, we justify the seemingly beneficial and appealing aspects of the idea.

A popular saying back in the 1960s was, "If it feels good, do it . . . and if you haven't tried it, don't knock it." Many people began to accept the idea that unless they had personal experience with something, they had no right to criticize it or call it a sin. Satan took that philosophy and couched it in even more subtle terms. Now we justify that it is acceptable to "try out an idea in our minds"— to identify with it in our thoughts. We don't have any real intention of engaging in the behavior, primarily because we don't want to be caught in the act by others. We justify to ourselves, however, that it just might be beneficial for us to try out a particular idea in our minds so we can see how we feel about it. We assume we will remain righteous in God's eyes if we never actually *do* in reality what we are *thinking* in our minds.

This faulty thinking has been around since the time of Adam and Eve. Jesus pointed to the danger of *identifying* with such thoughts and responding to them in the mind and heart: "You have heard that it was said to those of old, 'You shall not murder, and whoever murders will be in danger of the judgment.' But I say to you that whoever is angry with his brother without a cause shall be in danger of the judgment. . . . You have heard that it was said to those of old, 'You shall not commit adultery.' But I say to you that whoever looks at a woman to lust for her has already committed adultery with her in his heart (Matthew 5:21–22, 27–28).

Jesus taught the way we think is just as real as the way we behave. Sinning in our minds is just as real as sinning before the whole world. When we begin to identify with Satan's ideas, we are already in highly dangerous territory.

5. Why is it just as sinful to think about murder or adultery as it to commit these acts?

....

....

....

....

....

....

....

6. How could this same principle apply to other situations?

....

....

....

....

....

....

....

We Plot Out How to Act

Once we identify with the idea that Satan has planted in our mind, we begin to plot ways in which we might act it out. The more we identify with one of Satan's ideas, the stronger our desire grows to experience it. When that desire reaches a certain degree of intensity, we begin to make a plan for acting out the full-blown desire that began as only a prick of our imagination.

Let me give you a couple of examples. A man might start thinking about something he knows he cannot afford—perhaps an expensive new sports car. He thinks about how beautiful the car is and about all the benefits of owning it. Before long, he is thinking about how good it would feel to drive the car around town and how his friends would be impressed if he owned it. He imagines the car in front of his house and he fantasizes about driving it to work. Soon, he is making plans to go for a test drive at a local dealership.

Or maybe a woman begins to think about what it might be like to be married to a man with whom she works. The only problem is that he is already married. She ignores this fact and starts to think about all the benefits that might be associated with marrying him. She begins to see herself going places with him and starts to project how envious her friends would be. Before long, she is plotting a way to get this man to have lunch with her, in the hopes that she might find a way to get him to invite her out to dinner.

There is only a short step between having a strong *desire* for something and making a *plan* that puts that desire into action. Of course, in acting on such an idea, we rarely have an intent of turning it into a habit. We usually say, "I'm just going to try this one time to see what it's like." But if we try something we know to be sin, we are going to continue to desire it. We may try to convince ourselves that we are strong enough to say no to a second temptation—even though we were not strong enough to say no to the first temptation.

Once we make a decision to act out sin, we become self-deluded. We think we can control our fleshly tendencies, when in reality our fleshly tendencies are in control of us. When we give in to sin and it becomes a habit, we become addicted to our sin. It rules us. It dominates our every waking thought. It governs our every action.

Our natural human desires are strong, especially when they are coupled with our human will. Once we engage knowingly in sin, the desire for sin is even stronger and our will to sin is strengthened. We find it increasingly difficult to deny ourselves what we desire. Our willpower diminishes. Only as we trust the Holy Spirit to give us the power to withstand Satan's temptations can we turn away from sin and choose God's plan for good.

7. "For the good that I will to do, I do not do; but the evil I will not to do, that I practice. Now if I do what I will not to do, it is no longer I who do it, but sin that dwells in me" (Romans 7:19–20). When have you made a similar lament in your life?

8. "When desire has conceived, it gives birth to sin; and sin, when it is full-grown, brings forth death" (James 1:15). What does James imply is the danger in just "trying out" something that you know to be a sin?

ALL SIN BEGINS WITH SATAN'S IDEAS

The Holy Spirit and Satan both have access to our minds. We do not think thoughts totally on our own initiative. Our imaginations represent the soil in which the Holy Spirit plants seed-ideas that will bear a harvest of blessing. In like manner, Satan has been allowed to *attempt* to plant seeds that have no potential other than to become wild weeds of destruction.

We must choose to let the thoughts from God remain and take root in us. With great diligence, we must decide to let the thoughts that are from Satan fly right on by. We must refuse to entertain Satan's notions or to engage in fanciful imaginations about evil.

Peter gave us this wisdom about how we can avoid the devil's process of deception: "Be sober, be vigilant" (1 Peter 5:8). To be *sober* means to have a clear mind and not have any fuzzy thinking about what is right or wrong. We are to know with certainty God's commandments and Jesus' teachings so we will know instantly if an idea is from Satan or from the Holy Spirit. It is our responsibility to maintain a sober mind. No one else can read and study God's Word for us. We must set our minds to learn what is right and what is wrong from God's perspective.

To be sober also implies a seriousness about life. We are not to joke about the devil or take him lightly. We are to recognize that we have an enemy who wants only one thing: to wipe us out. If he can't wipe us out, he will settle for the next best thing: to render us ineffective and useless. We must take our enemy as seriously as he takes us.

To be *vigilant* means to be watchful, alert, and quick to say *no* to the devil. We do this by asking the Holy Spirit to help us stay vigilant. The devil has never pulled the wool over the eyes of the Holy Spirit. He has never deceived the One whom Jesus described as being the Spirit of Truth. Our vigilance is directly related to our reliance on the Holy Spirit to guide us in our daily decisions and choices. If we ask the Holy Spirit with a sincere heart to reveal to us the lies of the devil and to help us discern evil spirits at work, we can be assured that He will do so.

God never asked us to overcome the enemy on our own strength. However, we must choose to receive the Holy Spirit's help. Being sober and being vigilant mean being serious about following God in every area of our lives, twenty-four hours a day, every day of the year.

9. "Do not be conformed to this world, but be transformed by the renewing of your mind, that you may prove what is that good and acceptable and perfect will of God" (Romans 12:2). What does it mean to be conformed to this world? How does this happen?

_____

_____

_____

_____

_____

_____

_____

_____

_____

10. What does it mean to renew your mind? Why is a renewed mind essential if you want to understand the will of God?

_____

_____

_____

_____

_____

_____

_____

_____

TODAY AND TOMORROW

Today: The devil tries to turn my mind to evil, but the
Holy Spirit will turn it to good.

Tomorrow: I will ask the Lord to help me transform
my thinking this week.

CLOSING PRAYER

*Heavenly Father, we pray that you would make us ever more aware of the
enemy's tactics against us and surround us with Your marvelous hedge of protection. Allow Your angelic host to surround us and minister to us each and
every day as we confront trials and temptations. Enable us today, through
the work of Your Holy Spirit, to recognize when the enemy is seeking to plant
an idea into our imaginations so that we will never identify with that thought
or plot ways in which to act it out. We want only to serve and honor You
in everything that we say and do.*

NOTES AND
PRAYER REQUESTS

Use this space to write any key points, questions, or prayer requests from this week's study.

A POSTURE OF
ACTIVE RESISTANCE

IN THIS LESSON

Learning: If the devil is so powerful, how can I
hope to defeat him?

Growing: What is my role in this struggle,
and what is God's role?

Throughout history, we have many examples of people who re-
sisted evil in ways that were not militant, vengeful, or violent.
In fact, most of the Christian martyrs throughout the ages took
a stand against evil. In the Bible, we read how John the Baptist,
Stephen, and the disciple James were put to death for taking
a stand and proclaiming Jesus to be the Son of God. Early church
traditions also relate that Peter and Paul were put to death for

their faith, as were James (the brother of Jesus), Mark, Philip, Andrew, Jude, Bartholomew, and Thomas.

Each of these individuals—and many more who followed after them—steadfastly refused to deny the Lord Jesus, turn their backs on their faith, or expose their fellow Christians to harm. Their resistance made a difference in the world, and in the end Christ was proved victor. God's kingdom on earth expanded, while human-made kingdoms faded into history.

Resistance is the biblical approach to confronting and overcoming the devil. As Peter wrote, "Resist him, steadfast in the faith" (1 Peter 5:9). James echoed this teaching: "Submit to God. Resist the devil and he will flee from you. Draw near to God and He will draw near to you" (James 4:7–8). Both Peter and James make clear that we are to actively *resist* evil.

ACTIVE RESISTANCE

On the surface resistance may appear to be passive, but it is anything but passive in actual practice. Resistance is an active stance that is intentional and powerful.

Think about what you would do if you saw someone barreling directly toward you at a rapid pace. Imagine there is a sheer wall to your right and a sharp drop-off to your left. There is no way you can turn and outrun this adversary. What would you do? You would likely brace yourself for the hit. You would plant your feet squarely and lean forward, probably with one shoulder and leg a little ahead of your other leg and shoulder. You would grit your teeth, tense your muscles, and prepare for the blow, fully expecting that your adversary would bounce off you rather than knock you down. You are in a position of resistance.

Resistance is rowing against the tide of the culture and refusing to adopt evil practices, even though the people around us may be adopting them. Resistance is doing the right thing solely because it is the right thing to do. Resistance is saying no to offers and temptations that we know will lead us to a harmful place that we do not want to go. Resistance is first and foremost a firm decision to engage in the struggle against evil rather than backing off from attacks or retreating from the devil's advances.

1. "Therefore submit to God. Resist the devil and he will flee from you" (James 4:7). What does it mean to submit to God? To resist the devil? Give specific examples of each.

2. When have you deliberately chosen to resist evil? What were the circumstances? What were the results?

Resistance and Patience

Resistance takes strength and courage. It also takes patience. As James writes:

> Be patient, brethren, until the coming of the Lord. See how the farmer waits for the precious fruit of the earth, waiting patiently for it until it receives the early and latter rain. You also be patient. Establish your hearts (James 5:7–8).

We are to be patient with ourselves . . . and we are to be patient with our fellow believers. We must look with hope to the future that the Lord has for each one of us. God is doing a good work within us. He is doing a good work in the people around us—though perhaps in different ways and at a different pace. If we become impatient with our spiritual growth or the spiritual growth of others, we can become angry, frustrated, and unloving.

Such attitudes give an opportunity and foothold for Satan to do his work. These attitudes are ones of resistance. Resistance is *patient*.

3. "Love suffers long and is kind; love does not envy; love does not parade itself, is not puffed up" (1 Corinthians 13:4). What does it mean to parade oneself? What does it mean to be puffed up? How is love different from these attitudes?

....

....

....

....

....

....

....

....

4. How can envy make a person impatient with others? How does "suffering long" work to defeat envy?

....

....

....

....

....

....

....

....

....

....

RESISTANCE INVOLVES SUBMISSION TO GOD

Peter and James point to two words that are at the heart of our ability to resist the devil: *submission* to God and *faith*. *Submission* to God is saying, "I can't do this, but I know that You can." In our resistance against the devil, we might say, "I can't defeat the devil on my own, but with You, Lord, I can have the victory." This is certainly the position the apostle Paul took when he said, "I can do all things through Christ who strengthens me" (Philippians 4:13).

James described submission as developing a closer relationship to God. As he wrote, "Draw near to God and He will draw near to you" (James 4:8). The primary way to know God and to know how He wants us to overcome evil is to spend time with Him. After all, it is virtually impossible to have a close relationship with another person if we never communicate!

We draw near to God when we pray and read His Word. We draw near to Him when we set aside time solely to listen to Him and to wait on Him for direction and guidance. We draw near to the Lord when we periodically shut ourselves away with Him, closing off all other influences that might distract us from knowing Him better.

The closer we draw to God, the better we come to know Him. And the better we come to know Him, the more we witness His awesome power, experience His vast love, learn from His wisdom, and grow in our faith. We come to an even greater realization and conclusion: "Yes, God *can* defeat the devil on my behalf."

Those who submit their lives to God are humble. Humility and submission cannot be separated. The truly humble recognize they are totally dependent on God and that only God is God. Those who believe the truth about God with all of their hearts receive an abundant portion of God's grace. Again, the words of James, "But He gives more grace. Therefore He says: 'God resists the proud, but gives grace to the humble'" (James 4:6).

5. "Humble yourselves in the sight of the Lord, and He will lift you up" (James 4:10). What does it mean to humble yourself in the sight of the Lord? How is this done?

6. When have you deliberately humbled yourself in the past? What were the circumstances? What were the results?

RESISTANCE INVOLVES FAITH

Faith is also key in resisting the devil. It is saying to God, "I believe that You will." In our battle to overcome the enemy, our faith might be stated this way: "I believe that You will defeat the enemy and cause him to flee from me as I resist him and put my trust in You." In the Psalms, we find King David again and again making this kind of declaration of faith to the Lord:

- "O my God, *I trust in You*; let me not be ashamed; let not my enemies triumph over me" (25:2).
- "I have hated those who regard useless idols; but *I trust in the LORD*" (31:6).
- "You, O God, shall bring them down to the pit of destruction; bloodthirsty and deceitful men shall not live out half their days; *but I will trust in You*" (55:23).
- "Whenever I am afraid, *I will trust in You*" (56:3).
- "Cause me to hear Your lovingkindness in the morning, *for in You do I trust;* cause me to know the way in which I should walk" (143:8).

Each of us has been given a measure of faith from our birth (see Romans 12:3), but this does not mean we automatically have an active, vibrant, or mature faith. Our faith can lie dormant in us, for the most part unused. It also can remain a weak or immature faith. Jesus referred to both "great faith" and "little faith" (Matthew 6:30; 8:10, 26). The disciples asked specifically that Jesus increase their faith (see Luke 17:5). The implication from these passages in Scripture is clearly that our faith is capable of growth.

Our faith becomes alive and active when we recognize who we are in Christ. "Christ in me" is one of the most powerful statements of faith a person can make, for Christ has far greater power than any force of the devil (see 1 John 4:4). We grow in faith by using our faith and by trusting God in situation after situation, circumstance after circumstance, relationship after relationship. We develop a personal history in which we have been faithful in our obedience to God and He has been faithful in His loving care of us.

The Bible speaks frequently about walking in faith or standing in faith. *Faith is to be applied.* It is to be exercised and developed. When we stand in faith, we are saying, "I am fully persuaded that God is God, and I cannot be moved from that position." When we walk in faith, we are saying, "I have every confidence that God is with me wherever I am and that He will remain with me forever. I am fully convinced that He is working all things together for my eternal and highest good" (see Romans 8:28).

Remaining steadfast in our faith is an act of our will. We must *choose* to remain steadfast in faith—staying grounded, keeping our resolve, and refusing to give in to doubt or fear. The Holy Spirit will help us in this if we ask for His help. He is the One who gives us the power to endure the assault of the enemy against us . . . even to the last moment of our lives.

7. "But thanks be to God, who gives us the victory through our Lord Jesus Christ. Therefore, my beloved brethren, be steadfast, immovable, always abounding in the work of the Lord, knowing that your labor is not in vain in the Lord" (1 Corinthians 15:57–58). What does it mean to be *steadfast*? What does it mean to be *immovable*? Give examples of each.

....
....
....
....
....
....
....
....

8. Why is it important to understand that "your labor is not in vain in the Lord"? What does this phrase mean to you?

....
....
....
....
....
....
....
....
....
....

A CLOSE CONNECTION

In the battle against your adversary, your faith in Christ Jesus, your submission to God, and your resistance against the enemy are all closely connected. You can resist the devil only if your faith is strong. It will be impossible for you to resist the devil for very long if you do not believe that Christ Jesus in you can and will defeat the devil.

Furthermore, you can be firm in your faith only if you are completely submissive to God. This means that you are willing to submit all areas of your life to His control. When you do not submit an area to God, you are basically saying, "I can handle this. I don't need Your help." That is precisely the place where the devil will attack you! The good news is that God has given you a measure of faith to develop. You are capable of submitting to Him . . . and therefore you are capable of resisting the devil. When you do, he must flee.

9. "I beseech you therefore, brethren, by the mercies of God, that you present your bodies a living sacrifice, holy, acceptable to God, which is your reasonable service" (Romans 12:1). What does it mean to present your body as a living sacrifice to God? How is this done? Why is it "your reasonable service"?

10. What part does this "self-sacrifice" play in resisting the devil? In what ways must you stand firm with your body before you can resist the devil?

TODAY AND TOMORROW

Today: The Lord has promised that the devil will flee if I resist him.

Tomorrow: I will ask the Lord each day to show me how to actively resist the enemy.

CLOSING PRAYER

Lord God, we want to take a stance of active resistance against our enemy. Give us the wisdom to ask the right questions to see through his lies and the strength to stand strong even in the most intense times of temptation. Thank You for the example of people like Joseph in the Bible who assumed a posture of active resistance when attacked by the enemy. We see how You blessed Joseph as he stood firm in his resistance —how You elevated him to the role of prime minster of all of Egypt. Lord, had he succumbed even once to the temptations and enticements he experienced over time, he would have missed out on so much that You had planned for Him. Let his example serve as a model for us to follow and as an encouragement for the blessings that come in following Your will.

NOTES AND
PRAYER REQUESTS

. . . .

Use this space to write any key points, questions, or prayer requests
from this week's study.

Developing a Discerning Spirit

IN THIS LESSON

Learning: What does it mean to have a discerning spirit?

Growing: How can I attain discernment?

Many of God's people are in trouble today because they do not have a *discerning spirit*. They walk right into Satan's traps and never even know what happened to them. Once they find themselves in this place, they say, "I can't imagine what went wrong." Those who have a discerning spirit are able to point out these traps of Satan before they fall into them.

For this reason, each of us needs to develop a discerning spirit and teach our children how to have a discerning spirit as well. A discerning spirit is rooted in a knowledge of right and wrong. The time to begin teaching discernment—the difference between right and wrong—is not when the children have reached adulthood. We teach it to them from their early youth.

Moses told the Israelites they must thoroughly train their children in God's commandments. As he proclaimed, "These words which I command you today shall be in your heart. You shall teach them diligently to your children, and shall talk of them when you sit in your house, when you walk by the way, when you lie down, and when you rise up. You shall bind them as a sign on your hand, and they shall be as frontlets between your eyes. You shall write them on the doorposts of your house and on your gates" (Deuteronomy 6:6–9).

We must know right from wrong, both in theory and in practice. We must know how to apply God's truth to our lives and live in obedience to His commands. This is why Moses said we are to teach our children God's commandments *each* day, not just in a half-hour Sunday school lesson each week. We are to say to them, "This is right behavior, and this is wrong behavior. This is God's commandment, and this is the consequence of breaking God's commandment." An education in right and wrong must occur twenty-four hours a day, every day of the year.

Children who are thoroughly trained in God's commands—who have been taught right from wrong—have little trouble discerning Satan at work. They quickly pick up signals that tell them when things are not right. Their consciences are sensitive. Children who have not been taught right from wrong, on the other hand, become a slow-moving target for the enemy. Those who are allowed to do whatever they want, or who have been taught that everything is relative and there are no absolutes, will be easy prey for Satan.

1. "Everyone who partakes only of milk is unskilled in the word of righteousness, for he is a babe. But solid food belongs to those who are of full age, that is, those who by reason of use have their

senses exercised to discern both good and evil" (Hebrews 5:13–14). What do "milk" and "solid food" represent? What distinguishes "milk" from "solid food"?

....

....

....

....

....

....

....

....

2. According to these verses, what is needed to distinguish between good and evil?

....

....

....

....

....

....

....

....

....

THE IMPORTANCE OF KNOWING GOD'S PRINCIPLES

There have been times when I have entered a room full of people and immediately sensed in my spirit that something was not right. It was almost as if an inner alarm had gone off. At times, the room was even occupied by Christians, but my inner-spiritual radar told me something was amiss. In every case, I have discovered that this inner discernment was correct.

As a believer in Christ, you must be continually developing and exercising this kind of spiritual discernment. God does not want His people to live in darkness or to be without an ability to detect evil at work. For this reason, He has made every provision necessary for you to acquire and grow in your ability to discern your enemy. His provision is twofold: His *Word* and His *Spirit*. The Bible is your source-book for right and wrong, while God's Spirit is your teacher in helping you to choose good in your daily walk with Christ.

You grow in your knowledge of right and wrong only by remaining steadfastly in God's Word. If your parents did not teach you right from wrong at an early age, it is imperative that you retrain your mind. You can do this by reading God's Word on a consistent, daily basis. Believe what you read and accept God's Word at face value. God means what He says and says what He means. Apply what you read. Put God's Word to use by doing what it says.

God's Word will renew your mind as you read it, giving you insight into what He considers to be righteous and unrighteous behavior and attitudes. As you read God's Word on a daily basis, your very desires will begin to change. You will no longer feel drawn to or comfortable in harmful settings. You will develop a deep intuitive understanding that you simply do not belong in certain relationships.

Even if you had a wonderful Christ-centered childhood, you will benefit by staying in God's Word on a daily basis. What you have learned in the past will be reinforced in your mind and heart. A steady and consistent reading of God's commandments will help you keep from falling victim to false teachings and human philosophies.

3. "Guard what was committed to your trust, avoiding the profane and idle babblings and contradictions of what is falsely called knowledge—by professing it some have strayed concerning the faith" (1 Timothy 6:20–21). What is Paul referring to that has

been "committed to your trust"? What must be done for you to guard it?

....

....

....

....

....

....

....

....

4. What "profane and idle babblings and contradictions" does the world teach today? How does God's Word refute such teachings of the world?

....

....

....

....

....

....

....

....

....

THE SIMPLICITY OF THE TRUTH

Don't try to complicate or read your own meanings into God's Word. God has not made His Word too difficult for you to comprehend. You may benefit from a translation that presents God's truth in more modern English so you can better understand the language, but the *truths* of the Bible are quite plain. We are the ones who make the Bible complicated in our attempts to justify our own desire to sin or to explain away the passages that we find difficult to obey.

Paul warned the Corinthians that "as the serpent deceived Eve by his craftiness, so your minds may be corrupted from the simplicity that is in Christ" (2 Corinthians 11:3). Satan came to Eve in the Garden of Eden and asked, "Has God indeed said . . . ?" (Genesis 3:1). He planted a doubt in her mind. He implied that God might not actually have commanded Adam to refrain from eating the forbidden fruit—or perhaps that they had misinterpreted God's words.

As a result, Eve began to read into God's commandment more than God had actually said. She replied, "God has said, 'You shall not eat it, nor shall you touch it, lest you die'" (verse 3). Those were not God's exact words. The Lord had told Adam, "Of the tree of the knowledge of good and evil you shall not eat, for in the day that you eat of it you shall surely die" (2:17). Eve added something to God's Word.

Next, Satan tried to get Eve to believe that it would be good for her to eat the fruit of the tree because it would make her more like God. If she were more like God, she would not die, because God will never die. Satan complicated the message. He introduced confusion and questioning. If Eve had stayed obedient to God's plain and simple commandment, she would have been fine. The commandment was straightforward and easy to understand.

The same is true for virtually all of God's commandments. So, if you do not understand parts of the Bible, ask God to reveal what you need to know to live in a way that is pleasing to Him. The fact is that you may not need to have a full understanding of the depth of every verse in the Bible. Some of the information in the Bible is likely to be understood fully only after you are with the Lord in heaven. But you can be assured that God will reveal everything that you need to live a godly life each day. You can trust the Holy Spirit to teach you and remind you of the truth you need as you face specific situations and decisions.

5. "If any of you lacks wisdom, let him ask of God, who gives to all liberally and without reproach, and it will be given to him" (James

1:5). What are some areas of your life where you need God's wisdom right now? Make a list below.

....

....

....

....

....

....

6. What are some ways that you can ask God to provide that wisdom? Write out a prayer below and specifically ask Him to provide His guidance in these areas.

....

....

....

....

....

....

STAYING SENSITIVE TO OUR SURROUNDINGS

Much of what we take into our minds is of no eternal use. It has virtually no benefit in helping us live our daily lives. It serves as *clutter* and results in confusion. Instead, we need to turn to God's Word on a daily basis and turn *away* from the messages of the world. We need to refuse to listen to false teachers—those who may appear to be Christians but do not help us walk in close relationship with God. We must also refuse to listen to those who present messages that are impure, violent, rooted in greed, or portray humans as the center of the universe.

Likewise, we need to seek to be sensitive to our surroundings. Many Christians have suffered because they had no spiritual sensitivity as to what was happening in their world. We need to ask the Holy Spirit to help us remain alert and aware of both the opportunities and temptations that come our way. Throughout the Bible, we are admonished to *watch*.

In ancient times, watchmen were assigned to stand on the walls of fortified cities and serve as lookouts. They worked in shifts that provided round-the-clock coverage. Their responsibility was twofold: (1) watch for the approach of the enemy, and (2) watch for the approach of the king. Our role as discerning Christians today is the same. We are to watch for the Lord's appearance in our midst as much as we must be alert to the attacks of our enemy.

This means we must be continually alert for ways to share the gospel with others. We must be aware of what God wants to do in our lives as we serve as ambassadors for Christ. We must be on constant alert for opportunities to do good and to give encouragement to our fellow Christians. So ask the Lord to help you *watch*. He will quickly answer your prayer.

7. "Present yourself approved to God, a worker who does not need to be ashamed, rightly dividing the word of truth" (2 Timothy 2:15). What does it mean to be "rightly dividing the word of truth"? How do we present ourselves as "approved to God"?

8. "But the end of all things is at hand; therefore be serious and watchful in your prayers" (1 Peter 4:7). What does it mean to be serious in your prayers? To be watchful? Why are these things important in prayer?

....

....

....

....

....

REMAINING IN SUBMISSION TO GOD

The flip side of submission is *reliance*. When we are submitted to someone, we are at the same time reliant on that person. When we yield our personal defense to another person, we are reliant on that person to protect us. When we submit our ability to provide for ourselves, we are reliant on another person for our daily needs. When we submit to the decision-making authority of another person, we are reliant on that person to exercise wisdom on our behalf.

This is an important concept as it is related to spiritual discernment. With our finite mental ability, we simply cannot discern all the tactics of the devil. The devil is not omnipotent, but he is more powerful than any human being. The devil is not omniscient, but he knows more than any human being. The devil is not omnipresent, but he has been around longer than any human being. The devil has cunning tricks that are beyond our abilities to understand.

In order to exercise sound spiritual discernment, we must submit to God's authority and become reliant on His discerning power to work in us. Our submission to God includes submission to the authority of His Word. God expects us to do what He tells us, and as we obey His commandments, He takes on the responsibility for all of the consequences related to our obedience. When we trust

God's Word to be true, it is then up to God to be faithful to His Word and to perform what He has said He would do on our behalf.

Our submission to God also includes submission to the authority of the Holy Spirit. As believers in Christ, we are not abandoned to survive on our own in an evil world. But neither are we given free rein to do whatever we want to do. We are in a line of authority under God the Father, and the Holy Spirit is our immediate supervisor. Submission to and reliance on the Holy Spirit must be ongoing in our lives. It is a daily submission—not a one-time event.

In the end, our focus must be on God and His plans, purposes, and principles. When we are walking closely with the Holy Spirit, discernment will come naturally and quickly to us. This discernment is critical if we are to sidestep the traps the devil has set for us. In fact, discernment is the key to avoiding many of life's troubles and trials.

9. "You are all sons of light and sons of the day. We are not of the night nor of darkness. Therefore let us not sleep, as others do, but let us watch and be sober" (1 Thessalonians 5:5-6). What does it mean to be "sons of light" and "sons of the day"?

10. What responsibilities do these roles of sonship bring with them?

TODAY AND TOMORROW

Today: The Holy Spirit wants to give me more wisdom and discernment.

Tomorrow: I will ask the Lord each day this week to give me wisdom and discernment.

CLOSING PRAYER

Holy Spirit, we submit ourselves to You. We want to do only what You want us to do. We want to shun evil and pursue good. We are trusting You to reveal any sin in our lives and any error that we are about to make. We want to be totally reliant on You to show us which choice to make, which path to pursue, which opportunity to seize, which relationship to forge, and which call to answer. We are also reliant on You to reveal the presence of evil or attack of the devil on our lives and show how we might resist the devil and overcome him. Please help us today.

Notes and
Prayer Requests

Use this space to write any key points, questions, or prayer requests from this week's study.

ENGAGING IN WARFARE

IN THIS LESSON

Learning: Is there really a spiritual war going on today?

Growing: How can I fight someone that I can't even see?

No member of the military engages in warfare on his own initiative. Specific orders must come from those who have the authority to wage war. Even the President of the United States, the commander in chief of the military, cannot declare war without an act of Congress. In the body of Christ, we are under the authority of our spiritual commander in chief, Jesus Christ our Lord. He is the One who authorizes us to engage in warfare against the devil.

This is an important concept to understand. We *do* have the authority to fight the devil. That authority has been given to each of us by Jesus. At the same time, if Jesus had not given us that author-ity, we would have no basis on which to fight our enemy and no chance of overcoming him. Our battle orders against Satan come from Jesus and from Him alone. He is our commander in the battle. He is the One who fights on our behalf and wins the victory.

The Gospel of Matthew records an event in which the Pharisees, the Jewish religious leaders of the day, accused Jesus of casting out demons by the power of Beelzebub, the ruler of the demons. Jesus' response conveys an important message as we battle our adversary:

> Every kingdom divided against itself is brought to desola-tion, and every city or house divided against itself will not stand. If Satan casts out Satan, he is divided against him-self. How then will his kingdom stand? And if I cast out demons by Beelzebub, by whom do your sons cast them out? Therefore they shall be your judges. But if I cast out demons by the Spirit of God, surely the kingdom of God has come upon you. Or how can one enter a strong man's house and plunder his goods, unless he first binds the strong man? And then he will plunder his house. He who is not with Me is against Me, and he who does not gather with Me scatters abroad (Matthew 12:25–30).

Jesus told the Pharisees: (1) if Satan casts out Satan, he is divided against himself; (2) every kingdom divided against itself will not stand; and (3) if a person is not with Him in battling demonic power, then that person was against Him. If we are not *completely* with Jesus in battling our adversary—if we are relying on any other source of power apart from that of the Holy Spirit—we are actually working against Christ, and our efforts will fail.

We cannot defeat the devil using our intellect, our reasoning, or even our hatred of evil. We can only defeat the devil by relying on Jesus Christ to work in us and on our behalf. There is no successful warfare against the devil apart from Him. He authorizes our war against the devil, even as He empowers us to win it and gives us the courage to engage in it.

1. "He who is not with Me is against Me, and he who does not gather with Me scatters abroad" (Matthew 12:30). What is required to be *with* Jesus rather than *against* Him?

....

....

....

....

....

....

....

2. What does it mean to "gather with" Christ? How is this done in practical terms?

....

....

....

....

....

....

....

THE NEED FOR PERSEVERANCE IN THE STRUGGLE

We are assured of victory when we engage in warfare at Christ's command and under His authority. Given then, when it feels as if we are losing the battle, we need to keep two points in mind. *First, the loss of a battle is not the loss of the war.* We may lose a round in our fight against the devil and experience a setback.

When Jesus sent out His disciples to preach the gospel and heal the sick, He said if the people in a city did not receive them, they were to wipe the dust of that place from their feet, give a warning to the people, and move on (see Matthew 10:5–15). Jesus anticipated His disciples would not be successful all the time. Nevertheless, He expected them to move forward and do the maximum amount of good with the greatest amount of effectiveness. He expects the same of us. We are to do what He calls us to do. The results are His responsibility.

Second, the final victory will be revealed fully in eternity. We do not know the full impact that we have on the lives of others. Some of what we accomplish for Christ on earth will be revealed to us only in eternity. As believers in Christ, the devil has no hold on us. Nothing the devil can do to us will change our eternal destiny.

When Jesus sent out seventy of His disciples, two by two, He gave them specific instructions to preach the gospel and heal the sick, which included anything that might keep a person from being whole. The disciples returned to Jesus with great joy, saying, "Lord, even the demons are subject to us in Your name" (Luke 10:17). Jesus responded, "I saw Satan fall like lightning from heaven. Behold, I give you the authority to trample on serpents and scorpions, and over all the power of the enemy, and nothing shall by any means hurt you" (verses 18–19).

Throughout the Bible, *serpents* and *scorpions* are terms for demons. Jesus told His disciples then—and He tells us today—that His followers have authority over the devil and the devil can do nothing to cause eternal harm to those who call on the authority of Christ. We may get scared and feel pain from time to time, but we will not experience any eternal damage.

3. "Watch, stand fast in the faith, be brave, be strong. Let all that you do be done with love" (1 Corinthians 16:13–14). Why does Paul command you to be brave and strong? What role does your will play in being strong and courageous?

....

....

....

....

....

....

4. Why is courage important when facing the devil? What is the source of that courage?

....

....

....

....

....

....

How We Battle Our Adversary

The Bible reveals there are three things we are to do in battling our adversary. *First, we are to enter Satan's domain with boldness—but only after we have "bound the strong man."* When confronting the Pharisees, Jesus referred to the power it takes to enter a strong man's house (see Matthew 12:29). Jesus laid claim to all the power necessary to walk into the devil's domain, pick up those whom the devil had maimed or oppressed, and bring them out of the devil's prison. He could do this because He was able first to bind the devil.

If we are to likewise enter Satan's domain, we must first bind the strong man who holds power over a person—even if that person is us. We do this by keeping God's commandments, speaking God's words, and doing God's works. Keep in mind there are all types of bondage. Some people are bound today by habits they cannot seem to break. Others are bound in relationships with people who are committed to evil. The Word of God and the love of God's people are sufficient for breaking *all* types of bondage. There isn't a form of bondage that cannot be broken by the Lord— if we will say and do what the Lord requires of us.

Jesus said, "Whatever you bind on earth will be bound in heaven, and whatever you loose on earth will be loosed in heaven" (Matthew 18:18). We bind the forces of evil by praying against them and resisting them. We bottle them up, tie them up, and lock them up so they are "bound" in their efforts to tempt us or harm our eternal spirits. We then loose the force of God's saving love and grace on the earth by giving our witness for Christ Jesus, both in word and in deed, by loving others, and by forgiving those who have sinned against us.

Second, we are to limit the access that Satan has to our lives. The concept of "entering the strong man's house" is not limited to our moving into the devil's domain. The broader principle that Jesus taught includes the truth that we must not allow the devil entrance into our own house where he might cause us harm. As believers in Christ, we have the power to control our thoughts, what we put into our bodies, how we relate to people, and how we develop our faith and instill good spiritual disciplines. We can change our habits, perspectives, and attitudes.

Third, we are to remember that Jesus is present in the binding process of our adversary. Indeed, He is the One who does the binding. Jesus said to Peter, "On this rock I will build My church, and the gates of Hades shall not prevail against it. And I will give you the keys of the kingdom of heaven, and whatever you bind on earth will be bound in heaven, and whatever you loose on earth will be loosed in heaven" (Matthew 16:18–19).

The *rock* was Peter's great statement of faith: "You are the Christ, the Son of the living God" (verse 16). This is the central truth of our faith. The "gates of Hades" cannot defeat the church that teaches Jesus is the Son of the living God. In the time of Jesus, the gates of a city were the place of government and authority. All key decisions were made by those who sat in the city gates. Jesus was saying the power of the devil—the demonic authorities of hell itself—cannot win against a Christ-focused body of believers.

Jesus said He gives the "keys of the kingdom of heaven" to those who are in His church. When we hold the keys to a place, we determine who goes into it. We control the access. Again, the devil cannot enter an area of our lives unless we give him access to that area. Jesus assures us that what we do to bind the devil's power on earth is accomplished and sealed definitely and eternally in heaven. Anything that Jesus does has eternal consequences!

5. "Keep your heart with all diligence, for out of it spring the issues of life" (Proverbs 4:23). What does it mean to "keep your heart"? How is this done? Why is it so important?

6. "I will give you the keys of the kingdom of heaven, and whatever you bind on earth will be bound in heaven" (Matthew 16:19). What does it mean to *bind* and to *loose* something on earth?

7. What did Jesus mean when He gave His disciples the "keys to the kingdom of heaven"? How does this apply to you?

....

....

....

....

....

....

OUR SPIRITUAL ARMOR

Jesus taught there is great power in agreement. We are not to engage in spiritual warfare on our own. Rather, we are to live, work, give witness, and engage in warfare against our enemy as the *body* of Christ. Some spiritual battles may be personal. Nevertheless, it is important to find at least one other person to be a prayer partner as you resist the devil and pray for God's will in your life. We are likely to find we are able to engage in our battle with greater courage and bring the battle to an end more quickly if we ask for the prayers of others. God does not intend for us to battle against our enemy in isolation.

Nor has God left us defenseless. As the apostle Paul wrote, "We do not wrestle against flesh and blood, but against principalities, against powers, against the rulers of the darkness of this age, against spiritual hosts of wickedness in the heavenly places. Therefore take up the whole armor of God . . . having girded your waist with truth, having put on the breastplate of righteousness, and having shod your feet with the preparation of the gospel of peace; above all, taking the shield of faith with which you will be able to quench all the fiery darts of the wicked one. And take the helmet of salvation, and the sword of the Spirit, which is the word of God; praying always with all prayer and supplication in the Spirit, being watchful to this end with all perseverance and supplication for all the saints" (Ephesians 6:12–18).

Notice that Paul said *our warfare is spiritual*. We must never think our warfare is against a particular person or group. The evil that exists in our world has its origins in the spiritual realm, and we are to go directly to the source of the evil and do our fighting there. Also, *the armor that we put on is Christ*. Every piece of armor is directly related to Jesus. We are to put on the truth of Jesus, the righteousness of Jesus, the gospel of peace embodied in Jesus, faith in Jesus as God's Son, and the salvation that Jesus purchased for us. We are to pick up the Word of God—upon which Jesus based all His words—as if it were our sword.

Furthermore, *our posture in warfare is one of resistance*. Only one piece of the armor has an offensive use. Every other aspect is for our defense, so we might "withstand in the evil day" (verse 13), "quench the fiery darts of the wicked one" (verse 16), and be able "to stand" (verse 13). Finally, *once we have put on Christ, we are to pray*. Before we take any other action, we are to pray. Prayer is the first thing we must do anytime we are under attack by the enemy. We are to pray with perseverance—with enduring power—until God's supernatural power is released in us. We are to be watchful in our prayers, alert, and diligent. By putting on Christ, standing, and praying, we will be "strong in the Lord and in the power of His might" (verse 10). When we are strong in Christ, we cannot be defeated!

8. "But put on the Lord Jesus Christ, and make no provision for the flesh, to fulfill its lusts" (Romans 13:14). What does it mean to "put on Christ"? How is this done?

9. What does it mean to "make provision for the flesh"? How can you avoid this?

....

....

....

....

....

....

....

....

10. What does each piece of armor do that Paul lists in Ephesians 6:14–18? How are you using each piece in your life?

Piece of armor	How is it used?	How are you using it?
Belt		
Breastplate		
Shoes		
Shield		
Helmet		
Sword		

TODAY AND TOMORROW

Today: The devil is actively fighting against me, but God provides me with armor and power.

Tomorrow: I will ask the Lord to show me how to put on each piece of spiritual armor daily.

CLOSING PRAYER

Father, motivate us each day to put on the spiritual armor that You have provided. Each morning, before we even get out of bed, compel us to put on the helmet of salvation to protect our thinking. The breastplate of righteousness to protect us from operating out of our emotions. The loins—gird about with the truth of who we are in Christ—to protect us from the enemy's lies. Help us to shod our feet with the preparation of the gospel of peace and pick up the shield of faith to ward off the flaming missiles that Satan launches at us. Enable us to wield the sword of the Spirit—Your living Word— to serve as our protection as well as our weapon. And let us always be in prayer, seeking Your will and desiring to walk upright before You.

Notes and Prayer Requests

· ·

Use this space to write any key points, questions, or prayer requests from this week's study.

WHAT THE ENEMY HATES

IN THIS LESSON

Learning: What powers do I have to fight against Satan?

Growing: How do I use my spiritual weapons?

Have you ever avoided someone solely because you didn't like what that person had to say? Perhaps he or she used profane or filthy language that offended you. Or perhaps he or she always made negative comments. Some non-Christians dislike being around Christians because they don't like hearing about Jesus, God's love, the work of the church, or the ministry of the Holy Spirit. Each of us is uncomfortable around certain people because of what they talk about—and the devil is uncomfortable around Christians who talk about things that he hates. Three things that the devil specifically hates to hear are: (1) the name of Jesus, (2) the references to the shed blood of Jesus on the cross, and (3) the quoted Word of God.

THE NAME OF JESUS CHRIST

The book of Acts relates that Peter and John one day encountered a lame man asking for alms as they made their way to the temple in Jerusalem. This man had been unable to walk from birth, and each day he had to be carried to the temple gate to beg for money. Luke writes that when the man asked Peter and John for money, they said, "Look at us" (Acts 3:4). The man gave them his full attention, expecting that he would receive alms from them.

But instead, Peter turned to the man and said, "Silver and gold I do not have, but what I do have I give you: In the name of Jesus Christ of Nazareth, rise up and walk" (verse 6). The Scriptures tell us that Peter then took the man by his right hand and lifted him up, and the man's feet and ankle bones immediately received strength. He had never walked in his life, yet he was suddenly able to stand, walk, and leap about, all the while praising God!

Peter and John were doing what Jesus had told them to do. Jesus had said to His disciples on the night before His crucifixion, "Most assuredly, I say to you, whatever you ask the Father in My name He will give you. Until now you have asked nothing in My name. Ask, and you will receive, that your joy may be full" (John 16:23–24).

The name of Jesus is not something that we simply tack onto our prayers. Jesus gave to His disciples—including us—the "power of attorney" to use His name. When we pray "in the name of Jesus," we are praying as if Jesus Himself is praying. We are to pray what He would pray, asking for what He would request of His heavenly Father. A prayer that is truly in the name of Jesus is totally in line with God's Word and with God's will.

The name of Jesus embodies all of the power and majesty that are rightfully Jesus' alone. His name is higher than any other name, and His power is greater than that of any person or any demon. As Paul wrote, "Therefore God also has highly exalted Him and given Him the name which is above every name, that at the name of Jesus every knee should bow, of those in heaven, and of those on earth, and of those under the earth, and that every tongue should confess that Jesus Christ is Lord, to the glory of God the Father" (Philippians 2:9–11).

The name of Jesus is a constant reminder to the devil that he is not as powerful as Christ. He does not have the relationship with the Father that Jesus has, nor is he the rightful heir to all of heaven. The devil doesn't want to be reminded of those truths.

1. "Therefore God also has highly exalted Him and given Him the name which is above every name" (Philippians 2:9). What does it mean that the name of Jesus is "above every name"? If Jesus is Lord of all, what does this suggest about the devil's status?

2. "At the name of Jesus every knee should bow, of those in heaven, and of those on earth, and of those under the earth" (Philippians 2:10). What does it say about the character of Jesus that every knee shall bow at the mere mention of His name?

THE SHED BLOOD OF CHRIST

When we pray, we enter into the throne room of God solely on the basis that Jesus Christ died for our sins. Throughout the Bible, we find evidence that shed blood was the means that God provided for His children to be reconciled to Himself and to one another. For instance, after Adam and Eve sinned in the Garden of Eden, God shed the blood of animals and made coats of animal skins for them to wear. These coats were a consistent reminder to them that God alone was the Giver, Author, and Ruler of all life (see Genesis 3:21).

Later, when the Israelites were preparing to leave Egypt for the Promised Land, the Lord sent a series of plagues against Pharaoh and the Egyptians to secure His people's release. The final plague was the death of every firstborn—both people and livestock—in every home that did not have the blood of a lamb sprinkled on the doorposts. The angel of death passed through Egypt, but it did not touch the homes where the blood had been applied (see Exodus 12:1–30).

Again, God was making a provision for *life* through the shedding of blood. God's Law required that animals be sacrificed. The shedding of blood was the means of reconciliation between God and people (see Leviticus 14:12–13). Likewise, the shed blood of Jesus on the cross was God's act in providing forgiveness and reconciliation for those who would receive it. Jesus' death was the one *final* sacrifice for atonement. "This Man, after He had offered one sacrifice for sins forever, sat down at the right hand of God. . . . For by one offering He has perfected forever those who are being sanctified" (Hebrews 10:12, 14).

By His shed blood, Jesus purchased humankind's forgiveness from sin. His death was the new covenant . . . and His blood had been shed for many for the remission of sins (see Matthew 26:28). In this way, Jesus dealt a mortal blow to the devil. No longer would Satan have access to Him to tempt Him. No longer would Satan have opportunity to keep Him from fulfilling God's purposes. Satan became a defeated foe the moment that Jesus died on the cross.

In the shed blood of Jesus, we have the means for forgiveness and eternal life. We also have protection against our adversary, who is the agent of destruction and death. When we engage in spiritual warfare against the devil, we are wise to pray, "By the authority of Jesus Christ, and under the protection of His shed blood, I pray against Satan." The blood of Jesus is a terrible reminder to Satan that he lost his battle with Jesus and that he has no power over anything that Jesus purchased with the price of His own blood.

3. "You were not redeemed with corruptible things, like silver or gold, from your aimless conduct received by tradition from your fathers, but with the precious blood of Christ" (1 Peter 1:18–19). In what sense are silver and gold "corruptible things"? How did God purchase your life?

....

....

....

....

4. How is the blood of Christ incorruptible? Why was it necessary that Jesus' blood had to be shed to provide you remission of sins?

....

....

....

....

5. Why is it so important to understand that it was the blood of Christ that redeemed you? How does this fact give you power to defeat Satan?

....

....

....

....

THE QUOTED WORD OF GOD

The third thing the devil cannot stand to hear is the quoted Word of God. "The word of God is living and powerful, and sharper than any two-edged sword, piercing even to the division of soul and spirit, and of joints and marrow, and is a discerner of the thoughts and intents of the heart" (Hebrews 4:12). The Word of God is powerful. However, we need to be specific when we quote from it to battle the enemy, just as Jesus was specific when He was tempted by Satan:

> Now when the tempter came to Him, he said, "If You are the Son of God, command that these stones become bread."
>
> But He answered and said, "It is written, 'Man shall not live by bread alone, but by every word that proceeds from the mouth of God.'"
>
> Then the devil took Him up into the holy city, set Him on the pinnacle of the temple, and said to Him, "If You are the Son of God, throw Yourself down. For it is written: 'He shall give His angels charge over you,' and, 'In their hands they shall bear you up, lest you dash your foot against a stone.'"
>
> Jesus said to him, "It is written again, 'You shall not tempt the LORD your God.'"
>
> Again, the devil took Him up on an exceedingly high mountain, and showed Him all the kingdoms of the world and their glory. And he said to Him, "All these things I will give You if You will fall down and worship me."
>
> Then Jesus said to him, "Away with you, Satan! For it is written, 'You shall worship the LORD your God, and Him only you shall serve.'"
>
> Then the devil left him, and behold, angels came and ministered to Him (Matthew 4:3-11).

Notice that each time the devil tempted Jesus, the Lord responded with a specific passage from the Word of God. He did not rely on human opinion or a quote from a so-called expert on the subject. Nor did Jesus command the devil to do anything other than to depart from Him. Jesus quoted the Bible, and the power of the Scripture was sufficient in defeating Satan. If that method was good enough for Jesus, it should be good enough for you and me.

Note also that Jesus used passages from the Bible that related directly to each of Satan's temptations. He was precise in His use of the Scriptures. We must know the Bible if we want to use it with precision. We must be familiar with the truths of the Bible from cover to cover. Think of the Bible as a sharp two-edged sword or a gun filled with live ammunition. The verses in the Bible are powerful weapons to use as we command the devil to depart from us. The Word of God indeed is our weapon against the adversary (see Ephesians 6:17).

So, when you are quoting the Bible to the enemy, find a passage of the Bible that is directly related to the problem you are facing. Read that passage of Scripture aloud as part of your prayers. Voice your belief in God to act for good on your behalf.

6. "Your word is a lamp to my feet and a light to my path" (Psalm 119:105). How has the Bible served to guide your way in your life?

7. "The word of God is living and powerful, and sharper than any two-edged sword, piercing even to the division of soul and spirit" (Hebrews 4:12). How does the Word of God act like a weapon that you can wield against the enemy?

8. How are you using this weapon? Why is it important to quote *specific* passages of Scripture when battling against the devil?

....

....

....

....

....

BATTLING THE DEVIL WITH PURITY OF HEART

When we speak the name of Jesus or quote the Word of God, we must do so with a pure heart that is totally submitted to the Lord Jesus Christ. The name of Jesus is not a magical word. The blood of Jesus is not a secret formula. We must never use the name of Jesus or make a reference to His blood in a cavalier or joking manner. Our battle with the enemy is deadly serious. Our position in Christ is the most important aspect of our lives.

9. "Watch and pray, lest you enter into temptation" (Matthew 26:41). Why must you be vigilant against the devil? Why must you be watchful when doing battle against him?

....

....

....

....

....

....

....

10. What is a situation that you are facing in which you need to rely on the power of Jesus for victory? How will you use Scripture as a weapon to battle against your enemy?

....

....

....

....

....

....

....

TODAY AND TOMORROW

Today: My source of power against the devil is in the name of Jesus and His Word.

Tomorrow: I will take steps to actively memorize passages from the Bible this week.

CLOSING PRAYER

Heavenly Father, we thank You for giving us such simple strategies to employ in our fight against the devil. We will call on the name of Jesus, rely on the shed blood of Christ on the cross, and use Your Word as a weapon when the enemy comes our way . . . knowing that he will have no choice but to flee from us. Write on our hearts the importance of these strategies. Build a willingness within us to pray God-centered, Christ-centered, and Spirit-centered prayers whenever we are under attack—knowing that You always provide a way of escape.

Notes and Prayer Requests

Use this space to write any key points, questions, or prayer requests from this week's study.

Saying No to Satan's World Order

IN THIS LESSON

Learning: What exactly is the "world order"?

Growing: How are the world's priorities different from God's priorities?

In recent decades, people have spoken about a "new world order." They have generally been referring to the realignment of political power in the aftermath of the collapse of the Soviet Union. The Bible also speaks of a world order—but the word *new* is never applied to it.

The apostle John gives us a description of this world order when he writes, "Do not love the world or the things in the world. If anyone loves the world, the love of the Father is not in him. For all that is in the world—the lust of the flesh, the lust of the eyes, and the pride of life—is not of the Father but is of the world. And the world is passing away, and the lust of it; but he who does the will of God abides forever" (1 John 2:15–17).

John also states, "We know that we are of God, and the whole world lies under the sway of the wicked one" (5:19). The world order depicted in the Bible is not one in which Christians are to be involved. It is a world order established by our adversary. It is not eternal, but it is pervasive on the earth today. We must resist it and counteract it every day of our lives.

The good news is that we can! John holds out this hope: "For whatever is born of God overcomes the world. And this is the victory that has overcome the world—our faith. Who is he who overcomes the world, but he who believes that Jesus is the Son of God?" (5:4–5). Through Christ, we have the wisdom and strength to live in a way that is opposed to Satan's world order.

WHAT IS "THE WORLD"?

The Bible uses the word *world* in three ways. *First, it refers to the inhabited world, the sum of the nations.* Jesus said, "Go into all the world and preach the gospel to every creature" (Mark 16:15). He was sending His disciples into all the inhabited regions and nations of the world.

Second, world is used to describe the whole of humanity. John wrote, "For God so loved the world that He gave His only begotten Son, that whoever believes in Him should not perish but have everlasting life" (John 3:16). John was referring to all the people of the earth.

Third, world is used to refer to a system or order. In Ephesians 2:1–2, Paul wrote, "And you He made alive, who were dead in trespasses and sins, in which you once walked according to the course of this world, according to the prince of the power of the air, the spirit who now works in the sons of disobedience." Paul was referring to the way the cosmos operates.

The word *world* is used 185 times in the New Testament, 105 of which occur in the writings of John. John spent most of his ministry in cities located on the west coast of Turkey—cities that at the time were heavily Greek in culture and Roman in rule. John was aware that the life of Jesus was 180-degrees opposed to the normal ways of Greek and Roman cultures.

1. "Now we have received, not the spirit of the world, but the Spirit who is from God, that we might know the things that have been freely given to us by God" (1 Corinthians 2:12). What is the spirit of the world? How does it differ from the Spirit of God?

2. What things have been freely given to us by God? What things does the world offer?

THE COSMOS AND CURRENT WORLD ORDER

The word *cosmos* refers to an arrangement of things. It is a key concept in understanding the devil's world order. The devil has a design or "arrangement" that he desires to perpetuate on humanity. Every facet of life has an arrangement: politics, education, art, commerce, science, music. Each of these areas works in a particular way and functions under certain laws. These facets work together to create an even larger arrangement—a cosmos. The fact things are ordered is not what is wrong. It is the *way* in which things are arranged that is the concern.

God's plan for the *perfect world order* is found in Genesis 1–2. In that story, we read that Adam was given the responsibility for governing a perfect world in a perfect way. In this perfect cosmos, God was in charge and Adam and Eve were completely reliant on Him. They made only wise decisions, because they trusted God to tell them what to do and how to do it. They enjoyed a perfect relationship with God and with one another—without manipulation, corruption, or sin. Their relationship mirrored perfectly the relationship they had with God.

But this perfect world order collapsed when Adam and Eve sinned, and another world order was established. This world order included the influence of Satan and his ability to manipulate and control humanity. In this world order, Satan sought to be the ruler of the earth—the one on whom humans were reliant and depended on for all decisions.

Every variety of world order since the demise of the Garden of Eden has been structured on this same premise of Satan seeking to be in absolute charge of all humankind. He desires to be the sovereign world ruler. Of course, the natural laws of the earth—such as gravity—were established by God and cannot be violated without consequences that God also established. The unchanging laws of God include spiritual laws and laws related to the mind and emotions of humankind. However, the systems of this world—the organized power structures and the way they work—are largely under Satan's domain.

As John said, "the whole world lies under the sway of the wicked one" (1 John 5:19). God allows Satan's influence on the earth, but He also has placed a limitation on him. Jesus clearly expressed that limitation when He said, "Now is the judgment of this world; now the ruler of this world will be cast out. And I, if I am lifted up from the earth, will draw all peoples to Myself" (John 12:31–32).

Jesus was speaking of His ministry to heal the sick and the demon-possessed, as well as of His crucifixion on the cross. He was saying that those who believed in Him and accepted His sacrifice would no longer be in the grip of Satan. They would be free to live in total obedience to God. Therefore, they need not live as victims of Satan's world order. They would still live *in* the world, but their behavior and attitudes would not be *of* the world.

3. "I have given them Your word; and the world has hated them because they are not of the world, just as I am not of the world. I do not pray that You should take them out of the world, but that You should keep them from the evil one. They are not of the world, just as I am not of the world" (John 17:14–16). What did Jesus mean when He said He was "not of the world"? What does it mean to be "of the world"?

4. Why doesn't God remove Christians from the world when they are saved? What does He choose to do instead?

....

....

....

....

....

SATAN'S PLOYS AND LIES

Satan uses two main ploys to draw people to himself so they might live according to his design. *First, he makes his world order as attractive as possible.* Satan does everything he can to make his world order appealing—but that attractiveness fades. Nothing that is held out by Satan can remain attractive, because everything Satan controls is seeded with his own decay.

Second, Satan makes promises that he cannot keep. Satan promises things that will be pleasurable, beneficial, and worthy of our participation, but those promises are short-lived. They cannot be fulfilled because they are not grounded in God's eternal goodness. It is important to recognize Satan's purpose behind these ploys. He seeks our destruction, our demise, and our death. His tricks are just that: *tricks.* He does not want us to flourish, prosper, or be blessed. All he offers is an *illusion* of goodness. The realities of his world order are only deceit, confusion, pain, suffering, and despair.

We also must recognize that Satan is supremely self-centered. Everything he does is designed to magnify his self-serving power and his self-seeking glory. He is not interested in sharing what he has amassed with anyone else. He is only interested in duping people to give him their souls. In the end, everything that Satan offers ends up being terrible.

Satan governs his world order through three principal lies. *First, he says that we can be self-sufficient.* Satan's foremost lie appeals directly to our greatest fear (loss of control) and our biggest character flaw (pride). Satan's lie is, "You don't need God. You can make it on your own." God says, "You need a Source for your life. You are limited in your power, your wisdom, and your ability. Furthermore, you were born with a sin nature, and you need a Savior. I am your Source, and I have provided Jesus Christ to be your Savior."

Second, Satan says that the pursuit of pleasure is our purpose on earth. Satan's lie is that if it feels good, we must acquire it or participate in it. From Satan's standpoint, there are no illegitimate desires, and all of our lusts should be fulfilled. God says that our desires must be filled in righteous ways or we will suffer the consequences.

Third, Satan says that security exists in possessions. Satan's lie is that we can purchase adequate defense, social status, and self-esteem. He exalts *things* rather than relationships. God's truth is that only He is our defender, provider, and shield. We come to a true sense of our worth when we realize that God sent His only Son to die so that we might live. Any status we have is solely because God allows us to hold that position for the sake of His kingdom.

5. "What comes out of a man, that defiles a man. For from within, out of the heart of men, proceed evil thoughts, adulteries, fornications, murders, thefts, covetousness, wickedness, deceit, lewdness, an evil eye, blasphemy, pride, foolishness." (Mark 7:20–22). Why does Jesus say that all these sins originate within us? How do they all bring defilement?

6. "For what will it profit a man if he gains the whole world, and loses his own soul? Or what will a man give in exchange for his soul?" (Mark 8:36–37). How do the things of this world endanger your eternal soul? Give examples.

....

....

....

....

....

....

....

LIVING FREE OF SATAN'S WORLD ORDER

Note that each of Satan's lies places top priority on *self* and the *present*. Satan does not want us to have a concern for other people or for how our actions today might affect the future. Certainly, we can look at the world today and see that people are primarily concerned with themselves and not God. Today's generation lives for today.

Jesus offers us hope and assurance that we can be free of Satan's lies and live in truth. *Truth* is the key to staying out of the treachery of Satan's world order. God's commandments give us the most fruitful, beneficial, and blessed way to live. We live in truth and avoid Satan's world order when we know and obey God's statutes.

The truth of God is that Jesus purchased our freedom from Satan through His death on the cross—and we can live in that freedom every day. We live in truth and avoid Satan's world order when we accept Jesus as our Savior and rely on Him daily to deliver us from evil. We do not need to be like this world. We can be transformed into the image of Christ Jesus. We can choose to live in truth and avoid Satan's world order by asking the Holy Spirit to change our habits and our attitudes and make us more and more like Jesus.

7. "If you abide in My word, you are My disciples indeed. And you shall know the truth, and the truth shall make you free" (John 8:31–32). What does it mean to abide in God's Word?

....

....

....

....

....

....

8. In what ways does God's truth set you free? What sorts of bondage do the lies of the world bring about?

....

....

....

....

....

Our Responsibility to Live Godly Lives

Our responsibility as Christians is not to live a life that has the world's approval. Rather, the Bible tell us that we are to live godly lives, regardless of the cost. As Paul wrote, "The grace of God that brings salvation has appeared to all men, teaching us that, denying ungodliness and worldly lusts, we should live soberly, righteously, and godly in the present age" (Titus 2:11–12).

As Christians, we will never have the approval of the world, so we waste our time if we try to win it. Rather than seek the approval of the world, we need to recognize that we are to be a *light* to the world—a bright witness to the truth of God's love and saving grace. So refuse to compromise with the world order established by Satan.

Remember that you are called instead to be a citizen of God's heavenly kingdom, which is an eternal and perfect order.

9. "Therefore do not let sin reign in your mortal body, that you should obey it in its lusts. And do not present your members as instruments of unrighteousness to sin, but present yourselves to God as being alive from the dead, and your members as instruments of righteousness to God" (Romans 6:12–13). What does it mean to let sin reign in your body? What rights does a reigning monarch have over his subjects?

....

....

....

....

....

....

....

....

....

10. Why are you commanded to present yourself to God "as being alive from the dead"? What effect would death have on the lusts of your flesh?

....

....

....

....

....

....

....

....

....

TODAY AND TOMORROW

Today: The Lord wants me to live as a light in
this world, bringing glory to Him.

Tomorrow: I will ask the Lord to show me areas
where worldly thinking has taken root in my mind.

CLOSING PRAYER

Lord, thank You for giving us the privilege of making choices—for the gift of free will. But thank You also for giving us the Holy Spirit to enable us to follow Your commands and sound the alarm when we are moving in the wrong direction. Help us today to submit to the influence of the Holy Spirit's work in our lives so we can recognize when the system of the world—the system of the enemy—is attempting to influence us. Free our minds today from the order of the world. May we choose to focus our minds on things that are pure, righteous, good, holy, and sacred to God.

NOTES AND PRAYER REQUESTS

Use this space to write any key points, questions, or prayer requests from this week's study.

FACING THE SPIRIT OF ANTICHRIST

IN THIS LESSON

Learning: Who is the antichrist?

Growing: How can I recognize the lies of Satan?

Throughout history, ambitious individuals have risen to power to promote their own personal causes. They nearly always couch themselves as the answer to a particular problem or even as the savior of the world. By the time these people reach a certain level of prominence and power, godly people have searched the Scriptures and concluded they are not of Christ. In some cases, these same godly people conclude the leader in question was "the Antichrist." So far, they have been wrong. We have not yet experienced the Antichrist. When he does make his appearance, the entire world will know, for he will loudly proclaim his arrival.

A PERSON OR A SPIRIT?

People often wonder if the Antichrist is a person or a spirit. The answer is both. There will be a person whose doctrine and deeds will earn him the title of *Antichrist,* but there also is a prevailing spirit of antichrist at work in our world today. The Antichrist will be a real man who will assume a right to rule the world and be the embodiment of evil. He will be filled with and directed by Satan himself. In the book of Revelation, John refers to this man as "the Beast." He will manifest supernatural powers and exert global influence (see Revelation 13).

The antichrist is also a spirit at work in the world. The word *antichrist* appears only in the epistles of John. John's concern was far more with the *spirit* of antichrist, whom he regarded as Satan himself, than with the person who would one day be filled with Satan and dominate the world stage. John saw Christians as being in a real and present struggle with the devil, who sought to be a false christ—a substitute of the real Christ.

The prefix *anti* has two meanings. The first conveys the idea of *being in place of something.* The second conveys the idea of *being opposed to something.* Satan always seeks to be in place of Christ, and he is always opposed to Christ. He is *anti*-Christ in everything that he says and does. He is the ultimate representation of ideas and behaviors that are opposed to Jesus. Many people have operated in the spirit of antichrist. This type of spirit is not a demon. Rather, it is a philosophy, a mindset, and a way of thinking and behaving.

The Bible refers to several types of *spirit.* We each have a *human* spirit. Paul wrote, "The Spirit Himself bears witness with our spirit that we are children of God" (Romans 8:16). There is a spirit of the *world,* which is the prevailing philosophy of the world order we discussed in the last lesson. "Now we have received, not the spirit of the world, but the Spirit who is from God, that we might know the things that have been freely given to us by God" (1 Corinthians 2:12).

Paul and John also wrote about a pervasive spirit that characterizes *evil people.* In Ephesians 2:2, we read about the "prince of the power of the air, the spirit who now works in the sons of disobedience." John refers to "false prophets"—those who champion what is evil (1 John 4:1). Peter said, "There were also false prophets among the people, even as there will be false teachers among you, who will secretly bring in destructive heresies, even denying the Lord who bought them, and bring on themselves swift destruction" (2 Peter 2:1).

These people operate with an evil intent, speak things contrary to the will of God, and operate in the spirit of antichrist. Everything they say is opposed to Christ. Everything they do is an attempt to take over the place that rightfully belongs to Christ alone.

1. "But there were also false prophets among the people, even as there will be false teachers among you, who will secretly bring in destructive heresies, even denying the Lord who bought them, and bring on themselves swift destruction" (2 Peter 2:1). What are the dangers of listening to false teachers and false prophets?

2. "And many will follow their destructive ways, because of whom the way of truth will be blasphemed" (2 Peter 2:2). How do false teachings dishonor "the way of truth"?

103

OUR RESPONSIBILITY TO TEST THE SPIRITS

Jesus warned there would be people who would attempt to deceive His followers: "Take heed that no one deceives you. For many will come in My name, saying, 'I am the Christ,' and will deceive many. . . . false christs and false prophets will rise and show great signs and wonders to deceive, if possible, even the elect" (Matthew 24:4–5, 24). Paul also warned against those who would preach any gospel other than the gospel of Christ. He spoke of "false apostles, deceitful workers, transforming themselves into apostles of Christ" (2 Corinthians 11:13).

We are warned repeatedly throughout the Scriptures that we are never to accept people's messages as true on the basis of their personality, their appearance, their ability to communicate well, the number of people who follow them, the music or testimonials they present, or the promises they make. The only basis of accepting any teaching must be whether it is in complete agreement with the written Word of God.

We are to *test* the spirits against the criteria of God's Word—and specifically against the criteria of what is said about Jesus in God's Word. Any person who says Jesus is not God's Son come in the flesh, or who denies the sovereignty of Christ as the sole provision for salvation, is a false teacher (see 1 John 4:1–3). We also must be on guard that we do not buy into a person's teaching or testimony because he or she seems to be speaking the truth about one particular issue or concern.

We must consider always the whole counsel of God's Word. *Everything* a person says must be in line with God's Word . . . not just a portion.

3. "Beloved, do not believe every spirit, but test the spirits, whether they are of God; because many false prophets have gone out

into the world" (1 John 4:1). What does it mean to "test the spirits"? How is this done in practical terms?

....

....

....

....

....

4. What criteria should you use to determine whether a teaching is of God?

....

....

....

....

....

CHARACTERISTICS OF THOSE WITH FALSE SPIRITS

Those who are filled with the spirit of antichrist—the devil's own spirit—often have the following characteristics. *First, they are manipulative.* False teachers exploit others for their own gain. If allowed to amass power, they will drain all of the finances of those who follow them. They destroy the individuality of their followers, often requiring that their followers dress and act in highly prescribed ways.

Second, they promote sensuality. False teachers nearly always claim that sensuality is to be highly valued and sexual sins are permissible. Many cult leaders are advocates of blatant fornication and adultery.

Third, they secretly introduce destructive heresies. False teachers take a portion of God's Word and twist it into a form that seems reasonable to human desires. They hold out a principle about which people can say, "Yes, that is the way it *ought* to be." The trouble is the principle they proclaim is not what the Word of God holds to be truth.

Fourth, they exhibit personal materialism and greed. False teachers with an antichrist spirit nearly always surround themselves with great wealth. Peter said, "By covetousness they will exploit you with deceptive words" (2 Peter 2:3).

5. "Jesus said to him, 'I am the way, the truth, and the life. No one comes to the Father except through Me'" (John 14:6). False teachers today often proclaim there are many ways to approach God and experience salvation. How does the Word of God counter this particular claim?

6. "For the wages of sin is death, but the gift of God is eternal life in Christ Jesus our Lord" (Romans 6:23). Some claim that God would never send people to hell for refusing to believe in Jesus as their Savior. What does Paul say is the result of sin? What is the only way the Scriptures provide for receiving eternal life?

OUTCOME FOR THOSE WITH AN ANTICHRIST SPIRIT

The Bible gives us a fivefold progression for those who have an antichrist spirit. This progression is most evident in the life of the future antichrist world leader, called the Beast, but it is also the path that is followed by any person who allows himself or herself to be filled with Satan's spirit.

First, they display lawlessness. Those with an antichrist spirit have no regard for God's law. To the contrary, they ridicule God's law and dismiss its value. Those with an antichrist spirit also hold themselves to be above the laws that govern other people. They have little regard for order or justice. They rule according to their own whims and dictates. As Paul wrote, "The mystery of lawlessness is already at work; only He who now restrains will do so until He is taken out of the way.... The coming of the lawless one is according to the working of Satan, with all power, signs, and lying wonders" (2 Thessalonians 2:7, 9).

Second, they claim to be a deity. Those with an antichrist spirit claim special powers or wisdom—just as Satan does. They claim to have knowledge about God that the Lord hasn't revealed to others. At times, they will claim to be under God but on par with Jesus—the mindset is usually that Jesus was just a good man, a prophet, and there have been many such people. False prophets also claim Jesus was only *a* son of God, not *the* Son, and that people today can have as much authority and dominion as Jesus.

Paul addressed these lies directly: "There is no other God but one ... there is one God, the Father, of whom are all things, and we for Him; and one Lord Jesus Christ, through whom are all things, and through whom we live" (1 Corinthians 8:4, 6). We are called to become sons of God and joint heirs with Christ, yet we are always *under* Christ's authority. The Bible never claims that any person can do what Christ did or be what Christ is—the only begotten Son of God, the Savior of the world, the King of kings, and the Lord of lords.

Third, they seek to rule others. People who are filled with an antichrist spirit do not live in isolation. They recruit followers and build power structures. They long to manipulate, control, and rule over people. Their desire for power over other people is insatiable, though their outward demeanor may be one of false humility and gentleness. Jesus taught us to pray, "Yours is the kingdom and the power and the glory forever" (Matthew 6:13). Those who try to get you to ascribe to their absolute rulership, power, and glory have an antichrist spirit.

Fourth, they are a tool of Satan. Those with an antichrist spirit may appear to be the ones doing the ruling and teaching, but ultimately they are pawns in the hands of Satan. Satan gives a form of power to his followers, but it is the power described in Revelation 9:3: "To them was given power, as the scorpions of the earth have power." This is the power to sting, to inflict pain, to cause suffering, and to bring about loss, destruction, and devastation. Jesus taught, "Whoever commits sin is a slave of sin" (John 8:34). Those with an antichrist spirit may *think* they are acting of their own accord, but in reality they are victims of Satan.

Fifth, they are ultimately destroyed by God. God may allow those with an antichrist spirit to exert influence for a season, but He will ultimately remove them from the scene. Paul wrote, "What fruit did you have then in the things of which you are now ashamed? For the end of those things is death" (Romans 6:21). Nothing built by those with an antichrist spirit will survive for long. False religions and cults rise and fall. Only what is of Christ will last on this earth. Only those whom Christ redeems will live with God forever.

7. "The coming of the lawless one is according to the working of Satan, with all power, signs, and lying wonders, and with all unrighteous deception among those who perish, because they did not receive the love of the truth, that they might be saved" (2 Thessalonians 2:9–10). What tactics does Satan use to deceive people?

8. According to these verses, why are people deceived? What must a person do to avoid being deceived by the lie of antichrist?

....

....

....

....

....

THREE QUESTIONS TO ASK

If you believe you are facing a person who has a false spirit, there are three questions you should ask. *First, do you believe that Jesus was God?* Those who possess an antichrist spirit will hem and haw at the question. However, those who are true believers will say, "Jesus was God come in the flesh." As John said, "Every spirit that does not confess that Jesus Christ has come in the flesh is not of God" (1 John 4:3).

Second, what do you believe about humankind and about humanity's relationship to God? Those with an antichrist spirit will claim that humans are supreme. They will state that God is a nice idea that is valuable to people, but in the end He is humankind's creation. Others will claim that God exists to serve people. However, true believers will say, "Humans are valuable to God, but they are always subservient to God. Our role is to serve God."

Furthermore, those who possess an antichrist spirit will claim that humans have no need for salvation. They will state that if people desire to improve themselves, they are fully capable of doing so without any help from God. But true believers in Christ will proclaim, "People need salvation and are incapable of achieving it on their own. Salvation is a gift of God, freely made available through Jesus Christ to all who will believe."

Third, what do you believe about the Bible? Those with a spirit of antichrist will be opposed to hearing the Word of God and will have no interest in the things of God. They will dismiss the Bible's authenticity and authority. They will be opposed to any efforts to live a life in accordance with God's commandments. But true Christ-followers will say, "I believe the Bible is the Word of God. It presents the way that God wants me to live, think, feel, and believe."

When we ask these questions of a person, we must listen closely to the answers with spiritual ears. We must ask the Holy Spirit to alert us to anything that is contrary to God's Word. We can trust the Holy Spirit to prick our consciences so that we will be able to tell right from wrong. As John said, "By this we know the spirit of truth and the spirit of error" (1 John 4:6).

The spirit of antichrist is pervasive in our world today, but it can be confronted, challenged, and denied. We do not need to be victims of those who are operating according to Satan's dictates or who are filled with his spirit. We *can* overcome the enemy—if we will be committed to a persistent and unrelenting obedience to God's truth.

9. "For such are false apostles, deceitful workers, transforming themselves into apostles of Christ. And no wonder! For Satan himself transforms himself into an angel of light. Therefore it is no great thing if his ministers also transform themselves into ministers of righteousness, whose end will be according to their works" (2 Corinthians 11:13–15). How do false teachers present themselves? Why it is so important for believers to have discernment from the Holy Spirit to uncover their lies?

10. What are some false teachings that circulate today? How can asking these three questions help you to know the truth?

....

....

....

....

....

....

TODAY AND TOMORROW

Today: The spirit of antichrIst is active in the world today.

Tomorrow: I will guard against Satan's lies by immersing myself in God's Word.

CLOSING PRAYER

Heavenly Father, we know there is a spirit in the world that is opposed to You and everything that You want to accomplish in our lives. Give us discernment today to recognize those who are filled with such a spirit of antichrist. Let us see through their smooth-sounding words so we can recognize they are being manipulative. Let us not be persuaded by their arguments that promote sensuality and an "anything goes" mentality. Let us comprehend when they are speaking destructive heresies that will only lead us astray from Your Word. And let us see them for what they are—people interested in only their own wealth, goals, and pleasures. Grant us the wisdom to see through such individuals and protect us from error through Your Holy Spirit.

NOTES AND
PRAYER REQUESTS

Use this space to write any key points, questions, or prayer requests from this week's study.

CHOOSING FAITH OVER REASON AND EMOTION

IN THIS LESSON

Learning: Where do logic and emotions enter this battle?

Growing: What if I don't have enough faith to obey God?

When faced with any decision in life, we operate from one of three positions: *faith, reason,* or *emotion.* Faith flows from our spirit. God endows us with faith so we can make the right choices related to Him. Reason and emotion flow from our soul—what we often term "the mind and the heart." Humans experience thoughts and feelings in their souls.

Thoughts and feelings are not eternal. They are related directly to the information, perceptions, and physical sensations that we have at a certain moment in time. Because of this, our thoughts and feelings can vary according to time and circumstances. When faced with a situation, reason says, "This is what I *think* and what seems right to me." Emotion says, "This is how I *feel*, and I am going to go with my feelings." But faith says, "This is what *God* says."

Faith, reason, and emotion are all related. It is virtually impossible to separate them at times. However, it is important to note that when it comes the enemy of our souls, he never appeals to our faith—but only to our reason and emotions. Furthermore, he attempts to drive a wedge that separates faith from reason and emotions. When we honor God and obey Him, He works in our lives to bring our reason and emotions in line with our faith. However, when we obey the devil, we only end up fragmented and confused.

God is not opposed to us using our minds or expressing our feelings. He wants us to be reasonable and emotionally healthy people. His laws are reasonable and logical, and when we obey them, we will experience joy. However, God desires for us to reason *with* Him, not *apart* from Him. In fact, the Bible tells us that He invites us to reason with Him: "Come now, and let us reason together" (Isaiah 1:18). The very next verse describes the consequences to obedience and disobedience in this matter: "If you are willing and obedient, you shall eat the good of the land; but if you refuse and rebel, you shall be devoured by the sword" (verses 19–20).

God wants us to understand that His thoughts, plans, and methods are greater than our own. "My thoughts are not your thoughts, nor are your ways My ways . . . for as the heavens are higher than the earth, so are My ways higher than your ways, and My thoughts than your thoughts" (Isaiah 55:8–9). No matter how much we know about a situation, we cannot know as much as God knows about it. As much as we might love another person and desire good on his behalf, we cannot love that person as much as God does. We shortchange ourselves when we choose to rely solely on our human emotions and reasoning and do not submit them to God. And the devil delights anytime we deny God, ignore God, or fail to experience God's best.

1. "For as the heavens are higher than the earth, so are My ways higher than your ways" (Isaiah 55:9). Why do you think that God uses this comparison to describe how His ways compare with your ways?

2. How do God's ways compare with your ways? How do God's methods differ from the methods of humankind?

THE CONFLICT BETWEEN FAITH AND REASON

We first see the first conflict between faith and reason way back in the Garden of Eden. Satan took on the form of a beautiful and cunning serpent, and then came to Eve and said, "Has God indeed said, 'You shall not eat of every tree of the garden'?" (Genesis 3:1). Eve replied, "We may eat the fruit of the trees of the garden; but of the fruit of the tree which is in the midst of the garden, God has said, 'You shall not eat it, nor shall you touch it, lest you die'" (verses 2–3).

The serpent responded by saying, "You will not surely die. For God knows that in the day you eat of it your eyes will be opened, and you will be like God, knowing good and evil" (verses 4–5). Satan appealed to Eve's reasoning ability. He introduced doubt— perhaps God didn't really mean what He had said, or perhaps God was holding out on Eve and not giving her everything that was for her good. Eve made a decision based on her reasoning ability, not on her faith in God. Throughout history, humankind has continued to make Eve's mistake.

Today, this has led to a world that has no tolerance for God's absolutes—a world that challenges all notions of *truth* and declares it can never be known. People argue their case on an issue based solely on their emotions. They make public policies solely on the basis of logical reasoning. Their attitudes are often are rooted in the way they feel about an issue—and the more they argue their position, the more heated they become in their expression.

The alternative is to ask, "What does God say?" The biblical views on most issues of life are nearly always simple, straightforward, and easy to understand. God's commandments are not shrouded in mystery. Even a young child can understand the Ten Commandments. The problem is not that we do not know God's opinion—the problem is that we do not want to *obey* what God says. Whenever we know what to do and then fail to do it, we are in rebellion against God. This is a very dangerous position in which to find ourselves.

3. "Has God indeed said, 'You shall not eat of every tree of the garden'?" (Genesis 3:1). Eve had not yet been created when God

told Adam not to eat the forbidden fruit. What doubts was Satan trying to plant in her mind through this conversation?

....

....

....

....

....

4. "The law of the LORD is perfect, converting the soul; the testimony of the LORD is sure, making wise the simple; the statutes of the LORD are right, rejoicing the heart; the commandment of the LORD is pure, enlightening the eyes" (Psalm 19:7–8). In what ways have you found God's Word to be perfect, sure, simple, right, pure, and enlightening?

....

....

....

....

....

FAITH IS THE ONLY WAY TO KNOW GOD

The believers in Corinth had predominantly come from a Greek background and held logic in high regard. They were specialists in "the wisdom of man." But Paul said to them, "The message of the cross is foolishness to those who are perishing, but to us who are being saved it is the power of God. For it is written: 'I will destroy the wisdom of the wise, and bring to nothing the understanding of the prudent.' Where is the wise? Where is the scribe? Where is the disputer of this age? Has not God made foolish the wisdom of this world? . . . The foolishness of God is wiser than men, and the weakness of God is stronger than men" (1 Corinthians 1:18–20, 25).

We can never come to know God or understand Him through reasoning, because our human minds cannot comprehend God. Most religions of the world assume otherwise. They state that if we only hone the intellect so that it is sharp enough, we can analyze God and come to understand Him. This subjects the intellect to a performance criterion.

Every religious system and cult is based on performance—on meeting certain standards. A person is told what to do, for how long, and to what degree. But this method does not work when we are facing an infinite, omniscient, and omnipotent God. After all, how could we possibly know when we have done enough, learned enough, or achieved enough? There is no way a finite creature can know the expectations of an infinite God.

Only through faith can we come to understand God. We *believe* that God is just, righteous, merciful, loving, and forgiving *solely* on the basis that this is what He said about Himself. Faith is believing that God has resources and evidence that we cannot know. The cross will never make sense to those who are attempting to find a logical way to God. The cross will be repulsive to those who hope to "feel" their way into God's presence. Yet the cross is the means that God has chosen for the redemption of humankind. We must believe in God and believe that He knows best . . . and not only for us but for every other person.

5. Why is the message of the cross "foolishness" in the world's eyes? Why does the world persistently reject Jesus' teachings that He is the only way to salvation?

....

....

....

....

....

6. What is the "wisdom of this world"? How is it the opposite of God's Word?

....

....

....

....

....

....

GOD'S ILLOGICAL METHODS

God's laws and commandments are logical. However, the methods that God employs to enact His will often are not. Just consider a few stories from the Bible. In the book of Exodus, God tells Moses to lead thousands of His people into a wilderness area—to the edge of an uncrossable sea. Approaching the people from the rear are the powerful forces of the Egyptians, and they are intent on capturing the people and returning them to slavery. God tells Moses to put his rod into the water. He does so, and the people walk across on dry ground.

In the book of Joshua, God tells an army commander to have his troops circle the city of Jericho once a day for six days. On the seventh day, he is to circle the city seven times, after which his troops are to blow trumpets and shout. The commander obeys. When the trumpets are sounded and the shouts are voiced, the walls of the city tumble and a victory is won.

In the book of Daniel, we read of three young Jewish men who are told by the Babylonian king Nebuchadnezzar to bow to a statue made of gold. The king's edict states that if anyone refuses to bow, they will be thrown into a fiery furnace. Nonetheless, the three men refuse, and God allows them to be thrown into the furnace. They live through the experience, coming out of the fires without even the smell of smoke on their clothes.

In the book of Esther, we encounter a young woman who learns an order has been issued for the destruction of the Jewish race. She fast and prays, and then hosts two dinner parties for her husband, the Persian king, and her arch-enemy, named Haman. In the course of the second dinnertime conversation, she openly accuses her enemy. In the end, her own life is spared, along with the lives of her people.

Do any of these situations make any intellectual sense? No, they are contrary to logic and reasoning. Do any of these situations make sense in light of normal emotional responses? No, the normal emotional response would be to cave in to fear and seek an alternative plan. However, by faith Moses, Joshua, Shadrach, Meshach, Abed-Nego, and Esther scored mighty victories that brought glory to God. What God asked them to do was illogical and against normal human emotional response: put a rod into the water, march around a city and shout, be thrown into a fiery furnace, and prepare a couple of banquets. Yet these actions based solely on faith brought about good results for God's people and the elimination of God's enemies.

7. "Naaman, commander of the army of the king of Syria . . . was also a mighty man of valor, but a leper. . . . Naaman went with his horses and chariot, and he stood at the door of Elisha's house. And Elisha sent a messenger to him, saying, 'Go and wash in the Jordan seven times, and your flesh shall be restored to you, and you shall be clean'" (2 Kings 5:1, 9–10). Naaman had come to Elisha to seek healing for his leprosy. How did the "cure" that Elisha proposed defy human logic and reasoning?

8. "Naaman became furious, and went away and said. . . . "Are not the Abanah and the Pharpar, the rivers of Damascus, better than all the waters of Israel? Could I not wash in them and be clean?' . . . [yet] He went down and dipped seven times in the Jordan, according to the saying of the man of God; and his flesh was restored like the flesh of a little child, and he was clean" (2 Kings 5:11-12, 14). How did Namaan react to Elisha's words? What happened when he nonetheless followed this "illogical" course and obeyed God?

....

....

....

....

....

JOIN THE BATTLE!

When you seek to understand God through reason alone, your efforts will only blind you to God. As Paul wrote, "If our gospel is veiled, it is veiled to those who are perishing, whose minds the god of this age has blinded, who do not believe, lest the light of the gospel of the glory of Christ, who is the image of God, should shine on them" (2 Corinthians 4:3-4). The Bible will often not make sense to your rational mind. Instead, you must come to the conclusion the man with a sick child reached: "Lord, I believe; help my unbelief!" (Mark 9:24).

The devil will continually tempt you to justify your sins and reason away your faith. He will constantly entice you to respond to your emotions—especially fear, anger, and hatred—rather than with faith. Don't listen to him! Choose to respond with your faith. When you respond with faith in Jesus Christ, you put your adversary on the run.

As a believer in Christ, take the devil seriously—but do not be overwhelmed by him or give in to his temptations. Do not ignore him or dismiss him lightly—but face him, resist him, and use your faith to overcome him. You can take this stance only if you remain close to Christ, turn to the Holy Spirit daily for wisdom, courage, and direction, and choose to believe that you are God's forgiven child and the devil has no claim on your eternal spirit.

Others may pray for you, believe with you, and encourage you in the battle. But in the end, you cannot hide behind the faith of others. Facing the devil is something you must do if you are to grow in your relationship with God. Facing the devil exercises your personal faith. It is an act of personal obedience to God. It puts you in a position to receive all the blessings and rewards that God has for you. In Christ Jesus you *can* and *will* overcome the enemy. So engage in the battle and trust God today for a victorious life!

9. "If our gospel is veiled, it is veiled to those who are perishing, whose minds the god of this age has blinded, who do not believe" (2 Corinthians 4:3–4). Who is "the god of this age"? How does he blind the minds of people today? Give examples.

....

....

....

....

....

10. "Jesus said to him, 'If you can believe, all things are possible to him who believes.' Immediately the father of the child cried out and said with tears, 'Lord, I believe; help my unbelief!' (Mark 9:23–24). When have you felt like this man? How has God helped you in the past when you sensed your faith was weak?

....

....

....

....

....

TODAY AND TOMORROW

Today: The only way to fully know God is through faith.

Tomorrow: I will ask the Lord to strengthen my faith through His Word and Holy Spirit.

CLOSING PRAYER

Heavenly Father, we recognize that every single temptation we face . . . we face with You at our side. You walk with us through every single attack from the enemy and set Your divine limitation on them. You open the door of escape. Give us wisdom to be able to discern between Your voice and the voice of Satan. Give us the courage to say no to all of the pressures of Satan. And when we do succumb to relying on our emotions and reasoning instead of faith—and fall into sin—we pray that You will compel us not to remain in self-pity and self-accusation but get right back on track. We want to always be moving right along in the center of Your will.

NOTES AND PRAYER REQUESTS

Use this space to write any key points, questions, or prayer requests from this week's study.

WHY WE KEEP FAILING

Learning: Why do I continue to fail in resisting some temptations even when I try my best?

Growing: How can I avoid repeated failures in the future?

Here is a question that Christians have been dealing with and agonizing over for centuries: *Why is it that we yield to temptation even when we are trying to stop?* Have you asked that question? I am talking about situations where you have yielded before. You have already tasted the consequences—and you know that they are not going to be good. The immediate pleasure is just that . . . pleasing for a passing moment. You know in your heart, in your spirit, and in your mind that the ultimate consequence is going to be pain and suffering.

So why do you still give in to that temptation? Perhaps you've even promised God that you are not going to do it anymore. You pray and tell Him, with all the sincerity in your heart, that you have absolutely closed the door. You make all kinds of plans and promises—and then you turn around and give in to that same temptation again. Why does that keep happening?

There is an answer. There is a reason. In fact, there are four main reasons—which we are going to explore in this lesson. We fall repeatedly to temptation because: (1) we misunderstand the nature of temptation, (2) we refuse to fully surrender our lives to Christ, (3) we have a satanic stronghold, and (4) we deal with the symptoms instead of the root issues.

1. What are some temptations you deal with on a regular basis?

....

....

....

....

....

....

....

....

2. What are some obstacles you have identified that hinder you from dealing with temptation effectively?

....

....

....

....

....

....

....

....

MISUNDERSTANDING THE NATURE OF TEMPTATION

There is an interesting verse in 2 Corinthians that shines light on our inability to resist or defeat certain temptations. Paul was writing to the church in Corinth, and he said, "For if indeed I have forgiven anything, I have forgiven that one for your sakes in the presence of Christ, lest Satan should take advantage of us; for we are not ignorant of his devices" (2:10–11).

Notice the apostle Paul said that he and the believers were *not* ignorant of Satan's devices or schemes. *However, sometimes we are ignorant of the ways in which Satan works in our lives and seeks to attack us.* This ignorance can be one of the main reasons why we repeatedly fail in the face of specific temptations—why Satan continues to "take advantage of us."

For example, many Christians confuse the *temptation* to sin with the actual practice of sin. In other words, they believe the temptation itself is a sin. When I say "temptation," I am referring to the desire to do something we know is wrong. It is an urge—sometimes even a strong and sudden urge—to do something we know would result in sin, or to *not* do something that would prevent us from sinning. But this temptation itself is not sin. When we feel the temptation to lust or be greedy, we have not yet committed the sin of lust or greed. Even if we really want to give in to that temptation, the desire in and of itself is not a sin.

There is an easy way to demonstrate the separation between temptation and sin. The author of Hebrews writes, "For we do not have a High Priest who cannot sympathize with our weaknesses, but was in all points tempted as we are, yet without sin" (4:15). Jesus experienced every form of temptation, yet He did not sin. Therefore, the pull of temptation itself is not a sin.

Another misunderstanding we often carry is that people somehow "fall into sin" as a result of temptation. We have all likely heard people say, "Well, I was doing fabulously in my spiritual life and everything was great, but then all of a sudden I just fell into sin." We use that phrase as if temptation or sin were traps lying in the road that we somehow stumbled into without seeing them. We use that idea to communicate that our sin or our failure to resist temptation wasn't really our fault. We are the victim. We just "fell."

However, the truth is that we do not *fall* into temptation. In every single instance of temptation and sin, there is always a moment when we say *yes* or *no*. Temptation can feel strong. It can hit us suddenly and *almost* feel undeniable. But every time we sin, there is a moment when we cast a ballot—where we either yield to our desires or say *no* to Satan.

The apostle Paul revealed this truth when he wrote, "No temptation has overtaken you except such as is common to man; but God is faithful, who will not allow you to be tempted beyond what you are able, but with the temptation will also make the way of escape, that you may be able to bear it" (1 Corinthians 10:13). There is always a way out of temptation. Therefore, if we move from temptation to sin, we have made a choice.

Finally, many Christians believe that when they are finally spiritually mature—when they grow up in a spiritual sense—they will no longer be harassed by temptation. I wish this were true, but sadly it is not. In fact, the more spiritually mature you become, the greater a threat you are to Satan. And the greater the threat you represent to Satan, the more he is going to attack you—including attacking you through temptation. When the devil feels threatened by you, he is going to pump up the pressure and increase the intensity.

Remember the story of King David? He was a man whom the Bible states was after God's own heart, the victor in the battle against Goliath, and the author of many psalms and prayers. He was spiritually mature. Yet he experienced temptation many times in this life, which included his failure to resist temptation when he was walking along the rooftop and saw Bathsheba.

3. Which of the three misunderstandings mentioned above strikes you as most interesting or most important? Why?

....

....

....

....

....

....

4. Where have you misunderstood or even ignored the role of temptation in your life?

....

....

....

....

....

REFUSING TO SURRENDER OUR LIVES TO CHRIST

A second reason why Christians fail to resist temptation is because they have not fully surrendered their lives to Christ. Paul wrote, "I beseech you therefore, brethren, by the mercies of God, that you present your bodies a living sacrifice, holy, acceptable to God, which is your reasonable service. And do not be conformed to this world, but be transformed by the renewing of your mind" (Romans 12:1–2).

How do we avoid being conformed to the world and living according to everything the world values? How do we avoid the sinful choices held up by the world? By presenting ourselves to God as living sacrifices. This requires not just some of ourselves—not a little bit here and a little bit there—but our *entire* selves. The truth is that as long as we willingly withhold some area of our lives for ourselves and refuse to yield it to God, we will repeatedly fail in that area. We will repeatedly give in to temptation.

The reason why we so often refuse to yield control of our entire lives is fear. We are afraid that if we really let go—if we give control of everything about us over to God—He will not be able to meet our needs the way we would like them to be met. If we turn our lives over to God, we are no longer in control, which means we have to accept what He gives us rather than going out and taking hold of what we think we need.

Of course, this mindset is a lie. Paul tells us that we will receive "the perfect will of God" when we fully offer ourselves as living sacrifices. But the reality is that we value the ability to fulfill our own desires more than we value God's will. In fact, all sin is basically us choosing what is right for ourselves in spite of what God has said and done.

So, if you are dealing with an area of repeated failure when it comes to sin, ask yourself whether you have presented the issue to God. Have you completely handed it over to Him and allowed Him to have absolute control? If not, you will continue to fail.

5. How have you understood the process of surrendering your life over to God?

6. Are there areas that you have *not* fully surrendered to God?

....

....

....

....

....

....

....

THE PRESENCE OF
SATANIC STRONGHOLDS

A third reason as to why we may repeatedly fail in our struggle against temptation is the presence of satanic strongholds in our lives. As we discussed in a previous lesson, a *stronghold* is an area of weakness that allows Satan to establish a presence in our lives. Think of it as a fortified castle built right in our heart. It is a pocket of resistance right in the middle of our spiritual life. This could be a stronghold of fear, a stronghold of immorality, or a stronghold of greed. It could be a stronghold of bitterness or anger. But whatever it is, a stronghold can create such a grip on our lives that we repeatedly fail again and again in that area.

Have you identified at least one area in your life where you would say, "I am extremely vulnerable there"? Is there an area where you keep failing again and again? If so, you may well have identified a stronghold that Satan has established in your life. This can certainly explain why you would have a difficult time resisting temptation!

The next question, of course, is how to remove a stronghold once it has been established. *The first step is to acknowledge you have a problem.* Take ownership in your responsibility for that problem. While it is true that Satan is the one who built the stronghold, he would have been able to do so unless you opened the door.

He cannot establish a fortification unless you allow him to have a foothold and the time to build.

The next step is to identify the source of the stronghold. When did this start to be a problem in your life? What caused this to become an issue for you? Sometimes, a weakness might develop in your life based on what others have told you—especially when you were young. For example, if you had parents who did not pay much attention to you or were critical of you, it is understandable that you would struggle with finding self-confidence and self-worth. Other times, strongholds might develop when you begin to indulge in a thought that is rebellious toward God. Over time, these thoughts become a pattern, the patterns lead to sinful choices, the choices become habits, and the habits become strongholds.

The final step is to tear down the stronghold. If you can identify the source for your stronghold, or at least some contributing factors, you can tear it down using what Paul referred to as "the weapons of our warfare" (2 Corinthians 10:4). Remember, these weapons are supernatural. Specifically, you attack the stronghold by invoking the blood of Jesus Christ that was shed on the cross. You also pray in the name of Jesus Christ, which is intolerable to your enemy. And you attack and tear down strongholds through the power of the Holy Spirit, because "He who is in you is greater than he who is in the world" (1 John 4:4).

7. What are some past events or past choices that might have resulted in Satan establishing a stronghold in your life?

8. What are some practical ways that you will seek to tear down that stronghold?

....

....

....

....

....

....

DEALING WITH SYMPTOMS
INSTEAD OF ROOTS

The fourth reason we often repeatedly fail to resist temptation is that we are trying to deal with the symptoms of a problem rather than the true source. In reality, we will only begin to find victory over our temptation when we identify and address the roots of the issue. For example, think of those who struggle with overeating. They have done everything they can to change in this area and find the victory. They have read books. They have gone to seminars. They have set up accountability partners. They have many people praying for them.

What we need to understand is that *overeating* is not the root issue. What is the root issue will be specific for each person. Sometimes, a person may overeat because of insecurity, and he or she finds security and safety in food. Other times, people may overeat because they are angry. When they feel anger, eating gives them positive vibes that helps them to deal with that rage inside of them. Or the root cause of the problem could be loneliness. The point is that the problem of overeating cannot be fixed by focusing solely on food. We need to look deeper and uncover the root issue that caused the problem.

Or take the problem of lust—sexual immorality or indulgence. What is the root cause of this issue? Again, it could be caused by a number of things. One of them is rejection. It is not really sex or lust that the person wants—but to be accepted. The individual wants to be loved and feel cared for. So, sometimes the person will give himself or herself sexually to others in an effort to feel accepted. Or he or she will seek out multiple partners with the same goal.

The problem is this does not work. This is obvious, because no matter how many sexual experiences such a person has, that individual will still never feel satisfied. The person is always left looking for more. Pornography operates in a similar way. The physical experience of sex or lust never gives us what we need. So trying to battle against the sexual desire—"Lord, I promise I will never do that again"—does not lead to a solution because sex isn't the root of the problem. It is feeling rejected or lonely or angry.

Think about any other vice that people often fight against—alcohol, greed, lying, laziness, and so on. All of these are symptoms of a deeper need that is unmet. And that need is almost always our longing for a real and genuine connection with our Creator.

9. What are some symptoms that keep popping up in your life?

....

....

....

....

....

....

10. How might you go about uncovering the roots of these issues? Who can you speak with to help you?

....

....

....

....

....

....

TODAY AND TOMORROW

Today: I don't have to remain in the cycle of repeatedly failing when I'm confronted by temptation.

Tomorrow: I will work with the Holy Spirit to identify any strongholds that have hindered me from resisting temptation.

CLOSING PRAYER

Father, thank You again that You have limited our temptations and provided a pathway for our escape. We recognize today that our repeated failures are Your admonitions—Your signals to us—that something is deeply wrong in our lives. This is not simply a surface problem, but something deep inside of us that You want to heal, correct, and deliver us from . . . simply because You love us with all Your heart. Help us to identify those areas of weakness where Satan has established a stronghold and begin to deal with them—knowing that You will lead us to freedom as we do this.

NOTES AND
PRAYER REQUESTS

· ·

Use this space to write any key points, questions, or prayer requests from this week's study.

How to Keep Moving Forward

Learning: If I fail to resist temptation, what then?

Growing: How do I move forward after sinning in a way that helps me grow spiritually and glorify God?

We have now spent eleven lessons together focused on the theme of overcoming the plans the enemy has for your life. We have covered a lot of good ground when it comes to playing defense in our battles against temptation. We have gained a greater understanding of our enemy, of spiritual warfare, and of how to choose faith over emotions. However, as we saw in the previous session, even the most spiritually mature Christian will never attain perfection on this side of eternity. Sooner or later, we will fail. We will give in to temptation . . . and we will choose sin in rebellion against God.

So the questions need to be asked: *What then? How do we respond? How do we move on after such failure? How do we live in such a way that we can continue moving forward even when we experience setbacks?* These are the issues that we will discuss in this final session. We will do so by looking at one of the most famous failures in all of Scripture—when David sinned by pursuing Bathsheba and arranging for her husband's murder.

The Lord sent a prophet named Nathan to convict David of his sin. Nathan told David the story of two men—one rich and one poor. The rich man had many flocks and herds, but the poor man had only one lamb that was like a part of his family. One day, a traveler came to visit the rich man, and he needed to prepare a meal. But instead of taking a sheep from his vast flock, he took the poor man's lamb.

David was outraged and said, "As the Lord lives, the man who has done this shall surely die!" (2 Samuel 12:5). Nathan replied, "You are the man! Thus says the LORD God of Israel: 'I anointed you king over Israel, and I delivered you from the hand of Saul. I gave you your master's house and your master's wives into your keeping, and gave you the house of Israel and Judah. And if that had been too little, I also would have given you much more! Why have you despised the commandment of the Lord, to do evil in His sight?'" (verses 7–9).

David's response to that moment is instructive for any child of God who desires to live well even after a colossal failure.

1. Why do you think God had Nathan tell the story of the rich man and poor man to King David? How did this help David to realize the depth of his sin?

....

....

....

....

....

....

2. How do you typically respond spiritually after giving in to temptation?

....

....

....

....

....

....

REPENT

Immediately after Nathan made his announcement, King David admitted, "I have sinned against the LORD" (2 Samuel 12:13). He would go onto record his confession in Psalm 51:

> Have mercy upon me, O God,
> According to Your lovingkindness;
> According to the multitude of Your tender mercies,
> Blot out my transgressions.
> Wash me thoroughly from my iniquity,
> And cleanse me from my sin.
>
> For I acknowledge my transgressions,
> And my sin is always before me.
> Against You, You only, have I sinned,
> And done this evil in Your sight (verses 1-4)

The first step we must likewise take after sinning is to repent. This is a scary word to many people, but it is a necessary step for anyone looking to truly move forward after a mistake. In my experience, there are two kinds of repentance that Christians practice: *real* and *fake*. Or, to put it in more palatable terms, *incomplete* repentance and *complete* repentance. Incomplete repentance is when we express some level of sorrow for our sin, but everything stays on the surface. We say, "God, I am sorry for my sin. I know I should not have done that." It is the equivalent of telling someone, "I'm sorry that I got caught."

Incomplete repentance also carries the attitude of, "I will try to do better." Meaning, we would like to no longer struggle with a particular sin or area of weakness, but we don't really have a plan in mind to fight against that sin. We are not committed to actually changing anything in our lives. We are just sorry. Have you been there? I have. We all have. But it is important that we don't stay there.

Complete repentance—real repentance—is much different. Genuine repentance includes a genuine confession of guilt before God. By this I mean a deliberate, willful admission that we have rebelled against a holy God. This isn't feeling sorry. This is feeling *grief*. It is feeling the full weight and measure of our actions and their consequences for ourselves and others.

Notice that David's confession in Psalm 51 included a recognition that he had sinned against God. Yes, David certainly sinned against Bathsheba and her husband—that was known. But David both understood and expressed that his sin was not merely an action taken against two people but also a rebellion against God. It is also clear that David took full responsibility for his sin. He begged God to be made clean, purified, and restored.

This is the attitude and the actions we should take when we give in to temptation.

3. What stands out to you in David's confession?

....

....

....

....

....

....

4. When have you experienced a moment of true grief and true repentance over your sin?

....

....

....

....

....

....

ACCEPT FORGIVENESS

The second step to take after failing to resist temptation is to understand and accept the truth that God has already forgiven us. He has already forgiven every failure we have committed and ever will commit. When Jesus died on the cross, all sin from all humankind was placed on Him. This means Jesus has already borne the full impact and penalty of our sin. As a result, God never abandons us when we make mistakes. He never rejects us. He always forgives us because the penalty for our rebellion was satisfied long ago through Christ.

This is the reality, and for the most part we know those truths on an intellectual level. But sometimes we have a difficult time in believing them. We have a hard time living as if they are actually true. What I mean is that even though God has already forgiven us, we often do not forgive ourselves. Sometimes we choose to hold on to our guilt and our shame. We continue to live in the reality of our failure rather than accepting the payment that has already been made and moving forward in genuine repentance. Instead, we need to echo David's words: "Purge me with hyssop, and I shall be clean; wash me, and I shall be whiter than snow" (Psalm 51:7). When God forgives us, we are *forgiven*. When He washes us, we are clean.

One reason we may choose to hold on to our guilt is because we feel confused about the consequences of our actions. The Bible is clear that the reason God has given us standards—the reason He has placed His law on our hearts—is because sin damages us. It harms us, and God doesn't want to see His children harmed. Therefore, even though God forgives our sin, we still may face significant consequences for that sin. We still may face discipline from our Father.

In your own life, be careful not to confuse God's discipline or the natural consequences of your sin with the idea that God has not forgiven you or that He is angry with you. This is not the case. He *has* forgiven you, and you can keep moving forward if you accept His forgiveness and accept any consequences that come about as a result of your choices.

5. Do you find it easy or difficult to believe that God has forgiven every sin you have committed and ever will commit? Explain.

6. When have you experienced God's forgiveness in a poignant or powerful way?

ACCEPT GOD'S DISCIPLINE

The third step to take after failing to resist temptation is to accept God's discipline. I briefly mentioned this earlier, but it is worth exploring on a deeper level that God disciplines His children when they rebel against Him. He does this for their own good—so they will learn and grow rather than continuing to wallow in their rebellion.

As any wise parent knows, discipline is a form of needed correction. It doesn't indicate a lack of love or forgiveness on the part of the parents. In the same way, God's discipline indicates that He loves us even in the midst of our disobedience and desires better for us. By fully accepting His forgiveness—which was provided for us 2,000 years ago at Calvary—we can also accept the discipline and consequences of our sinful actions more readily and move toward more obedient and victorious living.

Just look again at the example of King David. After Nathan exposed his sins, God declared, "Now therefore, the sword shall never depart from your house, because you have despised Me, and have taken the wife of Uriah the Hittite to be your wife" (2 Samuel 12:10). God was displeased by David's actions, and if you read the second half of David's story in 2 Samuel, you will find that God's discipline came true in many ways. The sword never left David's household.

Note that when David sinned against God, he did not immediately confess and repent. Indeed, it was some time later, and only after Nathan questioned his behavior. I believe the severity of the discipline David experienced was a direct result of his failure to confess and repent quickly. But if we repent immediately, showing heartfelt conviction and taking responsibility for our actions, our discipline may be less than what it could have been.

Now, you might ask, "If God has forgiven me, then why would He still discipline me?" He does so because discipline is an act of love. Forgiveness says that God is not going to hold your sin against you—that He has wiped it out. But because He loves you, and because He doesn't want a harmful action repeated again, He still disciplines you. God wants to teach you a lesson through the mistake, build you up, make you an encouragement to others, and deepen your relationship with Himself so that you will become more valuable in service to Him.

At this point, you might be thinking, "God, You are loving me far too much!" All of us feel that way at times, but the truth remains whether it is light discipline or heavy discipline. God's correction is always an expression of love to help you lest you ruin and destroy yourself. As the author of Hebrews states, "For whom the LORD loves He chasens" (12:6). So, when you are seeking to move forward after a failure, you need to accept the discipline of God without complaining, realizing that it comes as an expression of unconditional love.

7. What are ways that God might discipline His people today?

8. When have you had an experience with God's discipline?

SEEK GODLY COUNSEL

The final step is to seek godly counsel when we continue to struggle with a point of weakness. There will be times when we will fail to resist temptation even though we are doing everything to avoid sin. In those moments, one of the wisest things we can do is find someone we trust who can offer us wise and godly counsel. We need someone who can help us understand what need inside of us is not being met that is resulting in us trying to meet that need in a way that is unholy before God.

Pray about such counsel. Search it out. If you cannot find someone as a friend who can offer godly wisdom and godly counsel, find a professional who can do so. Find someone who will help you sort through the mess within you until you understand why. Find someone who can encourage you. This may be difficult to do. But if you are too proud to ask for help, I can assure you that Satan will defeat you. If you are too proud to ask for help—especially when you have repeated failures—you are not going to receive help. Because if you could have figured it out on your own, you would have done so already.

Never be too proud to say, "God, I don't know what to do next." Don't be too proud to pray the same prayer as David: "Have mercy upon me, O God, according to Your lovingkindness; according to the multitude of Your tender mercies, blot out my transgressions. Wash me thoroughly from my iniquity, and cleanse me from my sin" (Psalm 51:1–2). In the same way, don't be too proud to say to someone you trust, "I am in trouble. I don't know what to do. I don't know why I keep failing. Would you help me to understand what is going on inside of me?" The stakes are too high for pride. The stakes are too high for self-reliance and stubbornness. If you need help . . . get help.

So, are you ready to stop the cycle of failure, guilt, and shame? Are you ready to keep moving forward toward everything God has for you? Yes, there will be times when you fail. I wish I could say that life will get to the point where you will never fail, but that is not true. The real question is how you will *respond* after you fail. You can be deceived and refuse to face the truth, which will result in you not experiencing everything that God has for you. Or you can move forward and become a valuable vessel of God's love, mercy, and grace.

This is a choice we all have to make. But my plea to you today is this: don't waste your failures. Profit from them. Learn to keep moving forward toward everything God has promised.

9. Do you feel comfortable or uncomfortable asking others to speak into your life? Explain.

....

....

....

....

....

10. Where could you go for godly counsel if you needed it today?

....

....

....

....

....

TODAY AND TOMORROW

Today: I have a choice about how to respond when I fail to resist temptation.

Tomorrow: I will choose to take whatever steps are necessary to keep moving forward toward God rather than wallowing in guilt and shame.

CLOSING PRAYER

Heavenly Father, sometimes it is so difficult for us to have to face up to ourselves and our own failings. Today, we pray that we will not run from the process that You have established for our restoration. May we always immediately repent when we choose to sin. May we accept the truth that You have already forgiven us. May we willingly accept Your discipline to correct us. And may we seek out godly counsel when we continue to struggle in an area of weakness. Take away our pride so that we can be used completely by You and for Your kingdom.

Notes and Prayer Requests

. . . .

Use this space to write any key points, questions, or prayer requests from this week's study.

LEADER'S GUIDE

Thank you for choosing to lead your group through this Bible study from Dr. Charles F. Stanley on *Overcoming the Enemy*. The rewards of being a leader are different from those of participating, and it is our prayer that your own walk with Jesus will be deepened by this experience. During the twelve lessons in this study, you will be helping your group members explore key themes about how to resist the devil's attacks through Dr. Stanley's teachings and review questions that will encourage group discussion. There are multiple components in this section that can help you structure your lessons and discussion time, so please be sure to read and consider each one.

BEFORE YOU BEGIN

Before your first meeting, make sure your group members each have a copy of *Overcoming the Enemy* so they can follow along in the study guide and have their answers written out ahead of time. Alternately, you can hand out the study guides at your first meeting and give the group members some time to look over the material and ask any preliminary questions. During your first meeting, be sure to send a sheet around the room and have the members write down their name, phone number, and email address so you can keep in touch with them during the week.

To ensure everyone has a chance to participate in the discussion, the ideal size for a group is around eight to ten people. If there are more than ten people, break up the bigger group into smaller subgroups. Make sure the members are committed to participating each week, as this will help create stability and help you better prepare the structure of the meeting.

At the beginning of each meeting, you may wish to start the group time by asking the group members to provide their initial reactions to the material they have read during the week. The goal is to just get the group members' preliminary thoughts—so encourage them at this point to keep their answers brief. Ideally, you want everyone in the group to get a chance to share some of their thoughts, so try to keep the responses to a minute or less.

Give the group members a chance to answer, but tell them to feel free to pass if they wish. With the rest of the study, it's generally not a good idea to have everyone answer every question—a free-flowing discussion is more desirable. But with the opening icebreaker questions, you can go around the circle. Encourage shy people to share, but don't force them. Also, try to keep any one person from dominating the discussion so everyone will have the opportunity to participate.

WEEKLY PREPARATION

As the group leader, there are a few things you can do to prepare for each meeting:

- *Be thoroughly familiar with the material in the lesson.* Make sure you understand the content of each lesson so you know how to structure the group time and are prepared to lead the group discussion.

- *Decide, ahead of time, which questions you want to discuss.* Depending on how much time you have each week, you may not be able to reflect on every question. Select specific questions that you feel will evoke the best discussion.

- *Take prayer requests.* At the end of your discussion, take prayer requests from your group members and then pray for one another.

- *Pray for your group.* Pray for your group members throughout the week and ask God to lead them as they study His Word.

- *Bring extra supplies to your meeting.* The members should bring their own pens for writing notes, but it's a good idea to have extras available for those who forget. You may also want to bring paper and additional Bibles.

STRUCTURING THE GROUP DISCUSSION TIME

You will need to determine with your group how long you want to meet each week so you can plan your time accordingly. Generally, most groups like to meet for either sixty minutes or ninety minutes, so you could use one of the following schedules:

SECTION	60 Minutes	90 Minutes
WELCOME (group members arrive and get settled)	5 minutes	10 minutes
ICEBREAKER (group members share their initial thoughts regarding the content in the lesson)	10 minutes	15 minutes
DISCUSSION (discuss the Bible study questions you selected ahead of time)	35 minutes	50 minutes
PRAYER/CLOSING (pray together as a group and dismiss)	10 minutes	15 minutes

As the group leader, it is up to you to keep track of the time and keep things moving according to your schedule. If your group is having a good discussion, don't feel the need to stop and move on to the next question. Remember, the purpose is to pull together ideas and share unique insights on the lesson. Encourage everyone to participate, but don't be concerned if certain group members are more quiet. They may just be internally reflecting on the questions and need time to process their ideas before they can share them.

GROUP DYNAMICS

Leading a group study can be a rewarding experience for you and your group members—but that doesn't mean there won't be challenges. Certain members may feel uncomfortable in discussing topics that they consider very personal and might be afraid of being called on. Some members might have disagreements on specific issues. To help prevent these scenarios, consider establishing the following ground rules:

- If someone has a question that may seem off topic, suggest that it is discussed at another time, or ask the group if they are okay with addressing that topic.

- If someone asks a question to which you do not know the answer, confess that you don't know and move on. If you feel comfortable, you can invite the other group members to give their opinions or share their comments based on personal experience.

- If you feel like a couple of people are talking much more than others, direct questions to people who may not have shared yet. You could even ask the more dominating members to help draw out the quiet ones.

- When there is a disagreement, encourage the members to process the matter in love. Invite members from opposing sides to evaluate their opinions and consider the ideas of the other members. Lead the group through Scripture that addresses the topic, and look for common ground.

When issues arise, encourage your group to follow these words from Scripture: "Love one another" (John 13:34), "If it is possible, as much as it depends on you, live peaceably with all men" (Romans 12:18), "Whatever things are true . . . noble . . . pure . . . lovely . . . if there is any virtue and if there is anything praiseworthy—meditate on these things" (Philippians 4:8), and "Be swift to hear, slow to speak, slow to wrath" (James 1:19). This will make your group time more rewarding and beneficial for everyone who attends.

Thank you again for your willingness to lead your group. May God reward your efforts and dedication, equip you to guide your group in the weeks ahead, and make your time together in *Overcoming the Enemy* fruitful for His kingdom.

Also Available in the
Charles F. Stanley Bible Study Series

The Charles F. Stanley Bible Study Series is a unique approach
to Bible study, incorporating biblical truth, personal insights,
emotional responses, and a call to action. Each study draws on
Dr. Stanley's many years of teaching the guiding principles found
in God's Word, showing how we can apply them in practical
ways to every situation we face. This edition of the series has
been completely revised and updated, and includes two
brand-new lessons from Dr. Stanley.

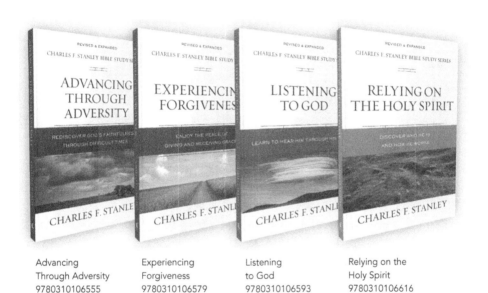

Advancing	Experiencing	Listening	Relying on the
Through Adversity	Forgiveness	to God	Holy Spirit
9780310106555	9780310106579	9780310106593	9780310106616

Available now at your favorite bookstore.
More volumes coming soon.

THOMAS NELSON
Since 1798